1 CORINTHIANS
A Life Application® Bible Study

1 CORINTHIANS
A LIFE APPLICATION® BIBLE STUDY

Part 1:
Complete text of 1 Corinthians with study notes from the
Life Application Study Bible
Part 2:
Thirteen lessons for individual or group study

Study questions written and edited by
Rev. Michael R. Marcey
Daryl J. Lucas
Rev. David R. Veerman
Dr. James C. Galvin
Dr. Bruce B. Barton

Tyndale House Publishers, Inc.
Wheaton, Illinois

Life Application Bible Studies

Matthew NIV	**1 Corinthians** NIV & NLT	**Hebrews** NIV
Mark NIV	**2 Corinthians** NIV	**James** NIV & NLT
Luke NIV	**Galatians & Ephesians** NIV & NLT	**1 & 2 Peter & Jude** NIV
John NIV & NLT	**Philippians & Colossians** NIV & NLT	**1 & 2 & 3 John** NIV
Acts NIV	**1 & 2 Thessalonians & Philemon** NIV	**Revelation** NIV & NLT
Romans NIV & NLT	**1 & 2 Timothy & Titus** NIV & NLT	

Visit Tyndale's exciting Web site at www.tyndale.com

Life Application Bible Studies: 1 Corinthians copyright © 1998 by Tyndale House Publishers, Inc., Wheaton, Illinois 60189. All rights reserved.

Cover photo copyright © 1998 by James McLoughlin. All rights reserved.

Life Application Notes and Bible Helps © 1986 owned by assignment by Tyndale House Publishers, Inc., Wheaton, Illinois 60189. Maps © 1986 by Tyndale House Publishers, Inc. All rights reserved.

Life Application is a registered trademark of Tyndale House Publishers, Inc.

The text of 1 Corinthians is from the *Holy Bible,* New Living Translation, copyright © 1996 by Tyndale Charitable Trust. All rights reserved.

ISBN 0-8423-3409-2

Printed in the United States of America

06 05 04 03 02
9 8 7 6 5 4 3

With 40 million copies in print, *The Living Bible* has been meeting a great need in people's hearts for more than thirty years. But even good things can be improved, so ninety evangelical scholars from various theological backgrounds and denominations were commissioned in 1989 to begin revising *The Living Bible.* The end result of this seven-year process is the *Holy Bible,* New Living Translation—a general-purpose translation that is accurate, easy to read, and excellent for study.

The goal of any Bible translation is to convey the meaning of the ancient Hebrew and Greek texts as accurately as possible to the modern reader. The New Living Translation is based on the most recent scholarship in the theory of translation. The challenge for the translators was to create a text that would make the same impact in the life of modern readers that the original text had for the original readers. In the New Living Translation, this is accomplished by translating entire thoughts (rather than just words) into natural, everyday English. The end result is a translation that is easy to read and understand and that accurately communicates the meaning of the original text.

We believe that this new translation, which combines the latest in scholarship with the best in translation style, will speak to your heart. We present the New Living Translation with the prayer that God will use it to speak his timeless truth to the church and to the world in a fresh, new way.

The Publishers
July 1996

Translation Philosophy and Methodology

There are two general theories or methods of Bible translation. The first has been called "formal equivalence." According to this theory, the translator attempts to render each word of the original language into the receptor language and seeks to preserve the original word order and sentence structure as much as possible. The second has been called "dynamic equivalence" or "functional equivalence." The goal of this translation theory is to produce in the receptor language the closest natural equivalent of the message expressed by the original-language text—both in meaning and in style. Such a translation attempts to have the same impact on modern readers as the original had on its own audience.

A dynamic-equivalence translation can also be called a thought-for-thought translation, as contrasted with a formal-equivalence or word-for-word translation. Of course, to translate the thought of the original language requires that the text be interpreted accurately and then be rendered in understandable idiom. So the goal of any thought-for-thought translation is to be both reliable and eminently readable. Thus, as a thought-for-thought translation, the New Living Translation seeks to be both exegetically accurate and idiomatically powerful.

In making a thought-for-thought translation, the translators must do their best to enter into the thought patterns of the ancient authors and to present the same ideas, connotations, and effects in the receptor language. In order to guard against personal biases and to ensure the accuracy of the message, a thought-for-thought translation should be created by a group of scholars who employ the best exegetical tools and who also understand the receptor language very well. With these concerns in mind, the Bible Translation Committee assigned each book of the Bible to three different scholars. Each scholar made a thorough review of the assigned book and submitted suggested revisions to the appropriate general reviewer. The general reviewer reviewed and summarized these suggestions and then proposed a first-draft revision of the text. This draft served as the basis for several additional phases of exegetical and stylistic committee review. Then the Bible Translation Committee jointly reviewed and approved every verse in the final translation.

A thought-for-thought translation prepared by a group of capable scholars has the potential to represent the intended meaning of the original text even more accurately than a word-for-word translation. This is illustrated by the various renderings of the Greek word *dikaiosune*. This term cannot be adequately translated by any single English word because it can connote human righteousness, God's righteousness, doing what is right, justice, being made right in God's sight, goodness, etc. The context—not the lexicon—must determine which English term is selected for translation.

The value of a thought-for-thought translation can be illustrated by comparing 2 Corinthians 9:1 in the King James Version, the New International Version, and the New Living Translation. "For as touching the ministering to the saints, it is superfluous for me to write to you" (KJV). "There is no need for me to write to you about this service to the saints" (NIV). "I really don't need to write to you about this gift for the Christians in Jerusalem" (NLT). Only the New Living Translation clearly translates the real meaning of the Greek idiom "service to the saints" into contemporary English.

Written to Be Read Aloud

It is evident in Scripture that the biblical documents were written to be read aloud, often in public worship (see Luke 4:16–20; 1 Timothy 4:13; Revelation 1:3). It is still the case today that more people will hear the Bible read aloud in church than are likely to read it for themselves. Therefore, a new translation must communicate with clarity and power when it is read aloud. For this reason, the New Living Translation is recommended as a Bible to be used for public reading. Its living language is not only easy to understand, but it also has an emotive quality that will make an impact on the listener.

The Texts behind the New Living Translation
The translators of the New Testament used the two standard editions of the Greek New Testament: the *Greek New Testament,* published by the United Bible Societies (fourth revised edition, 1993), and *Novum Testamentum Graece,* edited by Nestle and Aland (twenty-seventh edition, 1993). These two editions, which have the same text but differ in punctuation and textual notes, represent the best in modern textual scholarship.

Translation Issues
The translators have made a conscious effort to provide a text that can be easily understood by the average reader of modern English. To this end, we have used the vocabulary and language structures commonly used by the average person. The result is a translation of the Scriptures written generally at the reading level of a junior high school student. We have avoided using language that is likely to become quickly dated or that reflects a narrow subdialect of English, with the goal of making the New Living Translation as broadly useful as possible.

But our concern for readability goes beyond the concerns of vocabulary and sentence structure. We are also concerned about historical and cultural barriers to understanding the Bible, and we have sought to translate terms shrouded in history or culture in ways that can be immediately understood by the contemporary reader. Thus, our goal of easy readability expresses itself in a number of other ways:

- Rather than translating ancient weights and measures literally, which communicates little to the modern reader, we have expressed them by means of recognizable contemporary equivalents. We have converted ancient weights and measures to modern English (American) equivalents, and we have rendered the literal Greek measures, along with metric equivalents, in textual footnotes.

- Instead of translating ancient currency values literally, we have generally expressed them in terms of weights in precious metals. In some cases we have used other common terms to communicate the message effectively. For example, "three shekels of silver" might become "three silver coins" or "three pieces of silver" to convey the intended message. Again, a rendering of the literal Greek is given in textual footnotes.

- Since ancient references to the time of day differ from our modern methods of denoting time, we used renderings that are instantly understandable to the modern reader. Accordingly, we have rendered specific times of day by using approximate equivalents in terms of our common "o'clock" system. On occasion, translations such as "at dawn the next morning" or "as the sun began to set" have been used when the biblical reference is general.

- Many words in the original texts made sense to the original audience but communicate something quite different to the modern reader. In such cases, some liberty must be allowed in translation to communicate what was intended. Places identified by the term normally translated "city," for example, are often better identified as "towns" or "villages." Similarly, the term normally translated "mountain" is often better rendered "hill."

- Many words and phrases carry a great deal of cultural meaning that was obvious to the original readers but needs explanation in our own culture. For example, the phrase "they beat their breasts" (Luke 23:48) in ancient times meant that people were very upset. In our translation we chose to translate this phrase dynamically: "They went home *in deep sorrow.*" In some cases, however, we have simply illuminated the existing expression to make it immediately understandable. For example, we might have expanded the literal phrase to read "they beat their breasts *in sorrow.*"

- One challenge we faced was in determining how to translate accurately the ancient biblical text that was originally written in a context where male-oriented terms were used to refer to humanity generally. We needed to respect the nature of the ancient context while also trying to make the translation clear to a modern audience that tends to read male-oriented language as applying only to males. Often the original text, though using masculine nouns and pronouns, clearly intends that the message be applied to both men and women. One example is found in the New Testament epistles, where the believers are called "brothers" *(adelphoi).* Yet it is clear that these epistles were addressed to all the believers— male and female. Thus, we have usually translated this Greek word "brothers and sisters" in order to represent the historical situation more accurately.

  We have also been sensitive to passages where the text applies generally to human beings or to the human condition. In many instances we have used plural pronouns (they, them) in place of the masculine singular (he, him). For example, a traditional rendering of Proverbs 22:6 is: "Train up a child in the way he should go, and when he is old he will not turn from it." We have rendered it: "Teach your children to choose the right path, and when they are older, they will remain upon it." At times, we have also replaced third person pronouns with the second person to ensure clarity. A traditional rendering of Proverbs 26:27 is: "He who digs a pit will fall into it, and he who rolls a stone, it will come back on him." We have rendered it: "If you set a trap for others, you will get caught in it yourself. If you roll a boulder down on others, it will roll back on you." All such decisions were driven by the concern to reflect accurately the intended meaning of the original texts of Scripture.

  We should emphasize, however, that all masculine nouns and pronouns used to represent God (for example, "Father") have been maintained without exception. We believe that essential traits of God's revealed character can only be conveyed through the masculine language expressed in the original texts of Scripture.

Lexical Consistency in Terminology

For the sake of clarity, we have maintained lexical consistency in areas such as divine names, synoptic passages, rhetorical structures, and nontheological technical terms (i.e., liturgical, cultic, zoological, botanical, cultural, and legal terms). For theological terms, we have allowed a greater semantic range of acceptable English words or phrases for a single Greek word. We avoided weighty theological terms that do not readily communicate to many modern readers. For example, we avoided using words such as "justification," "sanctification," and "regeneration." In place of these words (which are carryovers from Latin), we provided renderings such as "we are made right with God," "we are made holy," and "we are born anew."

The Rendering of Divine Names

The Greek word *Christos* has been translated as "Messiah" when the context assumes a Jewish audience. When a Gentile audience can be assumed, *Christos* has been translated as "Christ." The Greek word *kurios* is consistently translated "Lord," except in four quotations of Psalm 110:1, where it is translated "LORD."

Textual Footnotes

The New Living Translation provides several kinds of textual footnotes:

- All Old Testament passages that are clearly quoted in the New Testament are identified in a textual footnote in the New Testament.

- Some textual footnotes provide cultural and historical information on places, things, and people in the Bible that are probably obscure to modern readers. Such notes should aid the reader in understanding the message of the text. For example, in Acts 12:1, "King Herod" is named in this translation as "King Herod

Agrippa" and is identified in a footnote as being "the nephew of Herod Antipas and a grandson of Herod the Great."

- When various ancient manuscripts contain different readings, these differences are often documented in footnotes. For instance, textual variants are footnoted when the variant reading is very familiar (usually through the King James Version). We have used footnotes when we have selected variant readings that differ from the Greek editions normally followed.

- Textual footnotes are also used to show alternative renderings. These are prefaced with the word "Or."

AS WE SUBMIT this translation of the Bible for publication, we recognize that any translation of the Scriptures is subject to limitations and imperfections. Anyone who has attempted to communicate the richness of God's Word into another language will realize it is impossible to make a perfect translation. Recognizing these limitations, we sought God's guidance and wisdom throughout this project. Now we pray that he will accept our efforts and use this translation for the benefit of the Church and of all people.

We pray that the New Living Translation will overcome some of the barriers of history, culture, and language that have kept people from reading and understanding God's Word. We hope that readers unfamiliar with the Bible will find the words clear and easy to understand, and that readers well versed in the Scriptures will gain a fresh perspective. We pray that readers will gain insight and wisdom for living, but most of all that they will meet the God of the Bible and be forever changed by knowing him.

The Bible Translation Committee
July 1996

The best way to define application is to first determine what it is *not.* Application is *not* just accumulating knowledge. Accumulating knowledge helps us discover and understand facts and concepts, but it stops there. History is filled with philosophers who knew what the Bible said but failed to apply it to their lives, keeping them from believing and changing. Many think that understanding is the end goal of Bible study, but it is really only the beginning.

Application is *not* just illustration. Illustration only tells us how someone else handled a similar situation. While we may empathize with that person, we still have little direction for our personal situation.

Application is *not* just making a passage "relevant." Making the Bible relevant only helps us to see that the same lessons that were true in Bible times are true today; it does not show us how to apply them to the problems and pressures of our individual lives.

What, then, is application? Application begins by knowing and understanding God's Word and its timeless truths. *But you cannot stop there.* If you do, God's Word may not change your life, and it may become dull, difficult, tedious, and tiring. A good application focuses the truth of God's Word, shows the reader what to do about what is being read, and motivates the reader to respond to what God is teaching. All three are essential to application.

Application is putting into practice what we already know (see Mark 4:24 and Hebrews 5:14) and answering the question, "So what?" by confronting us with the right questions and motivating us to take action (see 1 John 2:5, 6 and James 2:26). Application is deeply personal—unique for each individual. It is making a relevant truth a personal truth, and involves developing a strategy and action plan to live your life in harmony with the Bible. It is the biblical "how to" of life.

You may ask, "How can your application notes be relevant to my life?" Each application note has three parts: (1) an *explanation* that ties the note directly to the Scripture passage and sets up the truth that is being taught, (2) the *bridge* which explains the timeless truth and makes it relevant for today, (3) the *application* which shows you how to take the timeless truth and apply it to your personal situation. No note, by itself, can apply Scripture directly to your life. It can only teach, direct, lead, guide, inspire, recommend, and urge. It can give you the resources and direction you need to apply the Bible, but only you can take these resources and put them into practice.

A good note, therefore, should not only give you knowledge and understanding, but point you to application. Before you buy any kind of resource study Bible, you should evaluate the notes and ask the following questions: (1) Does the note contain enough information to help me understand the point of the Scripture passage? (2) Does the note assume I know more than I do? (3) Does the note avoid denominational bias? (4) Do the notes touch most of life's experiences? (5) Does the note help me apply God's Word?

WHY THE
LIFE APPLICATION STUDY BIBLE
IS UNIQUE

Have you ever opened your Bible and asked the following:

- What does this passage really mean?
- How does it apply to my life?
- Why does some of the Bible seem irrelevant?
- What do these ancient cultures have to do with today?
- I love God; why can't I understand what he is saying to me through his Word?
- What's going on in the lives of these Bible people?

Many Christians do not read the Bible regularly. Why? Because in the pressures of daily living they cannot find a connection between the timeless principles of Scripture and the ever-present problems of day-by-day living.

God urges us to apply his Word (Isaiah 42:23; 1 Corinthians 10:11; 2 Thessalonians 3:4), but too often we stop at accumulating Bible knowledge. This is why the *Life Application Study Bible* was developed—to show how to put into practice what we have learned.

Applying God's Word is a vital part of one's relationship with God; it is the evidence that we are obeying him. The difficulty in applying the Bible is not with the Bible itself, but with the reader's inability to bridge the gap between the past and present, the conceptual and practical. When we don't or can't do this, spiritual dryness, shallowness, and indifference are the results.

The words of Scripture itself cry out to us, "And remember, it is a message to obey, not just to listen to. If you don't obey, you are only fooling yourself" (James 1:22). The *Life Application Study Bible* does just that. Developed by an interdenominational team of pastors, scholars, family counselors, and a national organization dedicated to promoting God's Word and spreading the gospel, the *Life Application Study Bible* took many years to complete, and all the work was reviewed by several renowned theologians under the directorship of Dr. Kenneth Kantzer.

The *Life Application Study Bible* does what a good resource Bible should—it helps you understand the context of a passage, gives important background and historical information, explains difficult words and phrases, and helps you see the interrelationship of Scripture. But it does much more. The *Life Application Study Bible* goes deeper into God's Word, helping you discover the timeless truth being communicated, see the relevance for your life, and make a personal application. While some study Bibles attempt application, over 75 percent of this Bible is application-oriented. The notes answer the questions, "So what?" and "What does this passage mean to me, my family, my friends, my job, my neighborhood, my church, my country?"

Imagine reading a familiar passage of Scripture and gaining fresh insight, as if it were the first time you had ever read it. How much richer your life would be if you left each Bible reading with a new perspective and a small change for the better. A small change every day adds up to a changed life—and that is the very purpose of Scripture.

NOTES

In addition to providing the reader with many application notes, the *Life Application Study Bible* offers several explanatory notes that help the reader understand culture, history, context, difficult-to-understand passages, background, places, theological concepts, and the relationship of various passages in Scripture to other passages.

BOOK INTRODUCTIONS

The Book Introduction is divided into several easy-to-find parts:

Timeline. A guide that puts the Bible book into its historical setting. It lists the key events and the dates when they occurred.

Vital Statistics. A list of straight facts about the book—those pieces of information you need to know at a glance.

Overview. A summary of the book with general lessons and applications that can be learned from the book as a whole.

Blueprint. The outline of the book. It is printed in easy-to-understand language and is designed for easy memorization. To the right of each main heading is a key lesson that is taught in that particular section.

Megathemes. A section that gives the main themes of the Bible book, explains their significance, and then tells why they are still important for us today.

Map. If included, this shows the key places found in that book and retells the story of the book from a geographical perspective.

OUTLINE

The *Life Application Study Bible* has a new, custom-made outline that was designed specifically from an application point of view. Several unique features should be noted:

1. To avoid confusion and to aid memory work, the book outline has only three levels for headings. Main outline heads are marked with a capital letter. Subheads are marked by a number. Minor explanatory heads have no letter or number.

2. Each main outline head marked by a letter also has a brief paragraph below it summarizing the Bible text and offering a general application.

3. Parallel passages are listed where they apply.

PROFILE NOTES

Another unique feature of this Bible is the profiles of key Bible people, including their strengths and weaknesses, greatest accomplishments and mistakes, and key lessons from their lives.

MAPS

The *Life Application Study Bible* has a thorough and comprehensive Bible atlas built right into the book. There are two kinds of maps: a book introduction map, telling the story of the book, and thumbnail maps in the notes, plotting most geographic movements.

CHARTS AND DIAGRAMS

Many charts and diagrams are included to help the reader better visualize difficult concepts or relationships. Most charts not only present the needed information, but show the significance of the information as well.

CROSS-REFERENCES

An updated, exhaustive cross-reference system in the margins of the Bible text helps the reader find related passages quickly.

TEXTUAL NOTES

Directly related to the text of the New Living Translation, the textual notes provide explanations on certain wording in the translation, alternate translations, and information about readings in the ancient manuscripts.

HIGHLIGHTED NOTES

In each Bible study lesson you will be asked to read specific notes as part of your preparation. These notes have each been highlighted by a bullet (•) so that you can find them easily.

1 CORINTHIANS

1 CORINTHIANS

VITAL STATISTICS

PURPOSE:
To identify problems in the Corinthian church, to offer solutions, and to teach the believers how to live for Christ in a corrupt society

AUTHOR:
Paul

TO WHOM WRITTEN:
The church in Corinth and Christians everywhere

DATE WRITTEN:
Approximately A.D. 55, near the end of Paul's three-year ministry in Ephesus, during his third missionary journey

SETTING:
Corinth was a major cosmo-politan city, a seaport and major trade center—the most important city in Achaia. It was also filled with idolatry and immorality. The church was largely made up of Gentiles. Paul had established this church on his second missionary journey.

KEY VERSE:
"Now, dear brothers and sisters, I appeal to you by the authority of the Lord Jesus Christ to stop arguing among yourselves. Let there be real harmony so there won't be divisions in the church. I plead with you to be of one mind, united in thought and purpose" (1:10).

KEY PEOPLE:
Paul, Timothy, members of Chloe's household

KEY PLACES:
Worship meetings in Corinth

SPECIAL FEATURES:
This is a strong, straightforward letter.

ON A bed of grass, a chameleon's skin turns green. On the earth, it becomes brown. The animal changes to match the environment. Many creatures blend into nature with God-given camouflage suits to aid their survival. It's natural to fit in and adapt to the environment. But followers of Christ are *new creations,* born from above and changed from within, with values and lifestyles that confront the world and clash with accepted morals. True believers don't blend in very well.

The Christians in Corinth were struggling with their environment. Surrounded by corruption and every conceivable sin, they felt the pressure to adapt. They knew they were free in Christ, but what did this freedom mean? How should they view idols or sexuality? What should they do about marriage, women in the church, and the gifts of the Spirit? These were more than theoretical questions—the church was being undermined by immorality and spiritual immaturity. The believers' faith was being tried in the crucible of immoral Corinth, and some of them were failing the test.

Paul heard of their struggles and wrote this letter to address their problems, heal their divisions, and answer their questions. Paul confronted them with their sin and their need for corrective action and clear commitment to Christ.

After a brief introduction (1:1–9), Paul immediately turns to the question of unity (1:10—4:21). He emphasizes the clear and simple gospel message around which all believers should rally; he explains the role of church leaders; and he urges them to grow up in their faith.

Paul then deals with the immorality of certain church members and the issue of lawsuits among Christians (5:1—6:8). He tells them to exercise church discipline and to settle their internal matters themselves. Because so many of the problems in the Corinthian church involved sex, Paul denounces sexual sin in the strongest possible terms (6:9–20).

Next, Paul answers some questions that the Corinthians had. Because prostitution and immorality were pervasive, marriages in Corinth were in shambles, and Christians weren't sure how to react. Paul gives pointed and practical answers (7:1–40). Concerning the question of meat sacrificed to idols, Paul suggests that they show complete commitment to Christ and sensitivity to other believers, especially weaker brothers and sisters (8:1—11:2).

Paul goes on to talk about worship, and he carefully explains the role of women, the Lord's Supper, and spiritual gifts (11:3—14:40). Sandwiched in the middle of this section is his magnificent description of the greatest gift—love (chapter 13). Then Paul concludes with a discussion of the resurrection (15:1–58), some final thoughts, greetings, and a benediction (16:1–24).

In this letter Paul confronted the Corinthians about their sins and shortcomings. And 1 Corinthians calls all Christians to be careful not to blend in with the world and accept its values and lifestyles. We must live Christ-centered, blameless, loving lives that make a difference for God. As you read 1 Corinthians, examine your values in light of complete commitment to Christ.

THE BLUEPRINT

A. PAUL ADDRESSES CHURCH
   PROBLEMS
   (1:1—6:20)
   1. Divisions in the church
   2. Disorder in the church

Without Paul's presence, the Corinthian church had fallen into divisiveness and disorder. This resulted in many problems, which Paul addressed squarely. We must be concerned for unity and order in our local churches, but we should not mistake inactivity for order and cordiality for unity. We, too, must squarely address problems in our churches.

B. PAUL ANSWERS CHURCH
   QUESTIONS
   (7:1—16:24)
   1. Instruction on Christian marriage
   2. Instruction on Christian freedom
   3. Instruction on public worship
   4. Instruction on the Resurrection

The Corinthians had sent Paul a list of questions, and he answered them in a way meant to correct abuses in the church and to show how important it is that they live what they believe. Paul gives us a Christian approach to problem solving. He analyzed the problem thoroughly to uncover the underlying issue and then highlighted the biblical values that should guide our actions.

MEGATHEMES

THEME	EXPLANATION	IMPORTANCE
Loyalties	The Corinthians were rallying around various church leaders and teachers—Peter, Paul, and Apollos. These loyalties led to intellectual pride and created a spirit of division in the church.	Our loyalty to human leaders or human wisdom must never divide Christians into camps. We must care for our fellow believers, not fight with them. Your allegiance must be to Christ. Let him lead you.
Immorality	Paul received a report of uncorrected sexual sin in the church at Corinth. The people had grown indifferent to immorality. Others had misconceptions about marriage. We are to live morally, keeping our bodies for God's service at all times.	Christians must never compromise with sinful ideas and practices. We should not blend in with people around us. You must live up to God's standard of morality and not condone immoral behavior, even if society accepts it.
Freedom	Paul taught freedom of choice on practices not expressly forbidden in Scripture. Some believers felt certain actions—like eating the meat of animals used in pagan rituals—were corrupt by association. Others felt free to participate in such actions without feeling that they had sinned.	We are free in Christ, yet we must not abuse our Christian freedom by being inconsiderate and insensitive to others. We must never encourage others to do something they feel is wrong just because we have done it. Let love guide your behavior.
Worship	Paul addressed disorder in worship. People were taking the Lord's Supper without first confessing sin. There was misuse of spiritual gifts and confusion over women's roles in the church.	Worship must be carried out properly and in an orderly manner. Everything we do to worship God should be done in a manner worthy of his high honor. Make sure that worship is harmonious, useful, and edifying to all believers.
Resurrection	Some people denied that Christ rose from the dead. Others felt that people would not physically be resurrected. Christ's resurrection assures us that we will have new, living bodies after we die. The hope of the resurrection forms the secret of Christian confidence.	Since we will be raised again to life after we die, our life is not in vain. We must stay faithful to God in our morality and our service. We are to live today knowing we will spend eternity with Christ.

A. PAUL ADDRESSES CHURCH PROBLEMS (1:1—6:20)

Through various sources, Paul had received reports of problems in the Corinthian church, including jealousy, divisiveness, sexual immorality, and failure to discipline members. Churches today must also address the problems they face. We can learn a great deal by observing how Paul handled these delicate situations.

Greetings from Paul

1 This letter is from Paul, chosen by the will of God to be an apostle of Christ Jesus, and from our brother Sosthenes.

> **1:1**
> Acts 18:17
> Rom 1:1

²We are writing to the church of God in Corinth, you who have been called by God to be his own holy people. He made you holy by means of Christ Jesus, just as he did

> **1:2**
> Rom 8:28; 10:12-13
> 2 Tim 2:22

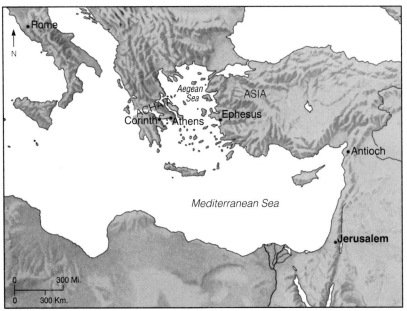

CORINTH AND EPHESUS Paul wrote this letter to Corinth during his three-year visit in Ephesus on his third missionary journey. The two cities sat across from each other on the Aegean Sea—both were busy and important ports. Titus may have carried this letter from Ephesus to Corinth (2 Corinthians 12:18).

● **1:1** Paul wrote this letter to the church in Corinth while he was visiting Ephesus during his third missionary journey (Acts 19:1–20:1). Corinth and Ephesus faced each other across the Aegean Sea. Paul knew the Corinthian church well because he had spent 18 months in Corinth during his second missionary journey (Acts 18:1-18). While in Ephesus, he had heard about problems in Corinth (1:11). About the same time, a delegation from the Corinthian church had visited Paul to ask his advice about their conflicts (16:17). Paul's purpose for writing was to correct those problems and to answer questions church members had asked in a previous letter (7:1).

● **1:1** Paul was given a special calling from God to preach about Jesus Christ. Each Christian has a job to do, a role to take, or a contribution to make. One assignment may seem more spectacular than another, but all are necessary to carry out God's greater plans for his church and for his world (12:12-27). Be available to God by placing your gifts at his service. Then as you discover what he calls you to do, be ready to do it.

● **1:1** Sosthenes may have been Paul's secretary who wrote down this letter as Paul dictated it. He was probably the Jewish synagogue leader in Corinth (Acts 18:17) who had been beaten during an attack on Paul and then later became a believer. Sosthenes was well known to the members of the Corinthian church, and so Paul included his familiar name in the opening of the letter.

1:2 Corinth, a giant cultural melting pot with a great diversity of

wealth, religions, and moral standards, had a reputation for being fiercely independent and as decadent as any city in the world. The Romans had destroyed Corinth in 146 B.C. after a rebellion. But in 46 B.C., the Roman emperor Julius Caesar rebuilt it because of its strategic seaport. By Paul's day (A.D. 50), the Romans had made Corinth the capital of Achaia (present-day Greece). It was a large city, offering Rome great profits through trade as well as the military protection of its ports. But the city's prosperity made it ripe for all sorts of corruption. Idolatry flourished, and there were more than a dozen pagan temples employing at least a thousand prostitutes. Corinth's reputation was such that prostitutes in other cities began to be called "Corinthian girls."

● **1:2** A personal invitation makes a person feel wanted and welcome. We are "called by God to be his own holy people." God personally invites us to be citizens of his eternal Kingdom. Jesus Christ, God's Son, is the only one who can bring us into this glorious Kingdom because he is the only one who removes our sins. "To be made holy" (or sanctified) means that we are chosen or set apart by Christ for his service. We accept God's invitation by accepting his Son, Jesus Christ, and by trusting in the work he did on the cross to forgive our sins.

1:2 This was probably not meant to be a private letter; rather, it may have been circulated to other churches in nearby cities. Although it deals with specific issues facing the church at Corinth, all believers can learn from it. The Corinthian church

all Christians everywhere—whoever calls upon the name of Jesus Christ, our Lord and theirs. ³May God our Father and the Lord Jesus Christ give you his grace and peace.

1:3
Rom 1:7

Paul Gives Thanks to God

1:5
2 Cor 8:7; 9:11

1:7
Rom 8:19, 23
Phil 3:20
2 Thes 1:7
Titus 2:13
2 Pet 3:12

1:8
Phil 1:6
1 Thes 3:13; 5:23

⁴I can never stop thanking God for all the generous gifts he has given you, now that you belong to Christ Jesus. ⁵He has enriched your church with the gifts of eloquence and every kind of knowledge. ⁶This shows that what I told you about Christ is true. ⁷Now you have every spiritual gift you need as you eagerly wait for the return of our Lord Jesus Christ. ⁸He will keep you strong right up to the end, and he will keep you free from all blame on the great day when our Lord Jesus Christ returns. ⁹God will surely do this for you, for he always does just what he says, and he is the one who invited you into this wonderful friendship with his Son, Jesus Christ our Lord.

1. Divisions in the church

1:10
Rom 15:5
1 Cor 11:18

¹⁰Now, dear brothers and sisters,* I appeal to you by the authority of the Lord Jesus Christ to stop arguing among yourselves. Let there be real harmony so there won't be divisions in the church. I plead with you to be of one mind, united in thought and purpose. ¹¹For some members of Chloe's household have told me about your arguments,

1:10 Greek *brothers;* also in 1:11, 26.

HIGHLIGHTS OF 1 CORINTHIANS	The Meaning of the Cross . . . . 1:18—2:16	Be considerate of one another because of what Christ has done for us. There is no place for pride or a know-it-all attitude. We are to have the mind of Christ.
	The Story of the Last Supper 11:23–29	The Last Supper is a time of reflection on Christ's final words to his disciples before he died on the cross; we must celebrate this in an orderly and correct manner.
	The Poem of Love 13:1–13	Love is to guide all we do. We have different gifts, abilities, likes, dislikes—but we are called, without exception, to love.
	The Christian's Destiny 15:42–58	We are promised by Christ, who died for us, that as he came back to life after death, so our perishable bodies will be exchanged for heavenly bodies. Then we will live and reign with Christ.

---

included a great cross section of believers—wealthy merchants, common laborers, former temple prostitutes, and middle-class families. Because of the wide diversity of people and backgrounds, Paul takes great pains to stress the need for both spiritual unity and Christlike character.

• **1:3** Grace is God's free gift of salvation given to us in Christ. Receiving it brings us peace (see Romans 5:1). In a world of noise, confusion, and relentless pressures, people long for peace. Many give up the search, thinking it impossible to find, but true peace of heart and mind is available to us through faith in Jesus Christ.

1:4-6 In this letter, Paul wrote some strong words to the Corinthians, but he began on a positive note of thanksgiving. He affirmed their privilege of belonging to the Lord and receiving his generous gifts: the power to speak out for him and understand his truth. When we must correct others, it helps to begin by affirming what God has already accomplished in them.

• **1:7** The Corinthian church members had all the spiritual gifts they needed to live the Christian life, to witness for Christ, and to stand against the paganism and immorality of Corinth. But instead of using what God had given them, they were arguing over which gifts were more important. Paul addresses this issue in depth in chapters 12–14.

• **1:7-9** Paul guaranteed the Corinthian believers that God would consider them "free from all blame" when Christ returns (see Ephesians 1:7-10). This guarantee was not because of their great gifts or their shining performance, but because of what Jesus Christ accomplished for them through his death and

resurrection. *All* who have received the Lord Jesus as their Savior will be considered blameless when he returns (see also 1 Thessalonians 3:13; Hebrews 9:28). If you have faith in Christ, even if it is weak, you *are* and *will be* saved.

1:10 Paul founded the church in Corinth on his second missionary journey. Eighteen months after he left, arguments and divisions arose, and some church members slipped back into an immoral life-style. Paul wrote this letter to address the problems and to clear up confusion about right and wrong so that they would remove the immorality from among them. The Corinthian people had a reputation for jumping from fad to fad; Paul wanted to keep Christianity from degenerating into just another fad.

1:10 By saying "brothers and sisters," Paul is emphasizing that all Christians are part of God's family. Believers share a unity that runs even deeper than that of blood brothers and sisters.

1:10, 11 To "let there be real harmony," allow for no "divisions" and "be of one mind, united in thought and purpose" does not require everyone to believe exactly the same. There is a difference between having opposing viewpoints and being divisive. A group of people will not completely agree on every issue, but they can work together harmoniously if they agree on what truly matters: Jesus Christ is Lord of all. In your church, speak and behave in a way that will reduce arguments and increase harmony. Petty differences should never divide Christians.

dear brothers and sisters. [12]Some of you are saying, "I am a follower of Paul." Others are saying, "I follow Apollos," or "I follow Peter,*" or "I follow only Christ." [13]Can Christ be divided into pieces?

Was I, Paul, crucified for you? Were any of you baptized in the name of Paul? [14]I thank God that I did not baptize any of you except Crispus and Gaius, [15]for now no one can say they were baptized in my name. [16](Oh yes, I also baptized the household of Stephanas. I don't remember baptizing anyone else.) [17]For Christ didn't send me to baptize, but to preach the Good News—and not with clever speeches and high-sounding ideas, for fear that the cross of Christ would lose its power.

The Wisdom of God

[18]I know very well how foolish the message of the cross sounds to those who are on the road to destruction. But we who are being saved recognize this message as the very power of God. [19]As the Scriptures say,

"I will destroy human wisdom
and discard their most brilliant ideas."*

[20]So where does this leave the philosophers, the scholars, and the world's brilliant debaters? God has made them all look foolish and has shown their wisdom to be useless nonsense. [21]Since God in his wisdom saw to it that the world would never find him through human wisdom, he has used our foolish preaching to save all who believe. [22]God's way seems foolish to the Jews because they want a sign from heaven to prove it is true. And it is foolish to the Greeks because they believe only what agrees with their own wisdom. [23]So when we preach that Christ was crucified, the Jews are offended, and the Gentiles say it's all nonsense. [24]But to those called by God to salvation, both Jews and Gentiles,* Christ is the mighty power of God and the wonderful wisdom of God.

1:12 Greek *Cephas.*   **1:19** Isa 29:14.   **1:24** Greek *Greeks.*

1:12
John 1:42
Acts 18:24
1 Cor 3:4

1:14
Acts 18:8; 19:29
Rom 16:23

1:17
Matt 28:19
John 4:2
Acts 26:17
2 Cor 10:10; 11:16

1:18
Rom 1:16
1 Cor 2:14
2 Cor 2:15; 4:3

1:19
†Isa 29:14

1:20
Job 12:17
Isa 19:11-12;
33:18; 44:25
1 Cor 2:6, 8

1:21
Matt 11:25

1:22
Matt 12:38

1:23
1 Cor 2:2

1:24
Col 2:3

1:12ff In this large and diverse Corinthian church, the believers favored different preachers. Because there was as yet no written New Testament, the believers depended heavily on preaching and teaching for spiritual insight into the meaning of the Old Testament. Some followed Paul, who had founded their church; some who had heard Peter in Jerusalem followed him; others listened only to Apollos, an eloquent and popular preacher who had had a dynamic ministry in Corinth (Acts 18:24; 19:1). Although these three preachers were united in their message, their personalities attracted different people. At this time the church was in danger of dividing. By mentioning Jesus Christ 10 times in the first 10 verses, Paul makes it clear who it is all preachers and teachers should emphasize. God's message is much more important than any human messenger.

1:12, 13 Paul wondered whether the Corinthians' quarrels had "divided" Christ into pieces. This is a graphic picture of what happens when the church (the body of Christ) is divided. With the many churches and styles of worship available today, we could get caught up in the same game of "my preacher is better than yours!" To do so would divide Christ again. But Christ is not divided, and his true followers should not allow anything to divide them. Don't let your appreciation for any teacher, preacher, or author lead you into pride. Our allegiance must be to Christ and to the unity that he desires.

1:17 When Paul said that Christ didn't send him to baptize, he wasn't minimizing the importance of baptism. Baptism was commanded by Jesus himself (Matthew 28:19) and practiced by the early church (Acts 2:41). Paul was emphasizing that no one person should do everything. Paul's gift was preaching, and that's what he did. Christian ministry should be a team effort; no preacher or teacher is a complete link between God and people, and no individual can do all that the apostles did. We must be content to operate within the gifts God has given us, and carry out his plan wholeheartedly. (For more on different gifts, see chapters 12 and 13.)

1:17 Some speakers use impressive words, but they are weak on content. Paul stressed solid content and practical help for his listeners. He wanted them to be impressed with his *message,* not just his style (see 2:1-5). You don't need to be a great speaker with a large vocabulary to share the Good News effectively. The persuasive power is in the story, not the storyteller. Paul was not against those who carefully prepare what they say (see 2:6) but against those who try to impress others with their knowledge or speaking ability.

• **1:19** Paul summarizes Isaiah 29:14 to emphasize a point Jesus often made: God's way of thinking is not like the world's way (normal human wisdom). And God offers eternal life, which the world can never give. We can spend a lifetime accumulating wisdom and yet never learn how to have a personal relationship with God. We must come to the crucified and risen Christ to receive eternal life and the joy of a personal relationship with our Savior.

• **1:22-24** Many Jews considered the Good News of Jesus Christ to be foolish, because they thought the Messiah would be a conquering king accompanied by signs and miracles. Jesus had not restored David's throne as they expected. Besides, he was executed as a criminal, and how could a criminal be a savior? Greeks, too, considered the Good News foolish: They did not believe in a bodily resurrection, they did not see in Jesus powerful characteristics of their mythological gods, and they thought no reputable person would be crucified. To them, death was defeat, not victory.

The Good News of Jesus Christ still sounds foolish to many. Our society worships power, influence, and wealth. Jesus came as a humble, poor servant, and he offers his Kingdom to those who have faith, not to those who do all kinds of good deeds to try to earn salvation. This looks foolish to the world, but Christ is the mighty power of God, the only way we can be saved. Knowing Christ personally is the greatest wisdom anyone can have.

1:25
2 Cor 13:4

1:26
Matt 11:25
John 7:48
Jas 2:1-5

1:27
1 Cor 3:18-19

1:28
Rom 4:17

1:29
Eph 2:9

1:30
Jer 23:5-6
Rom 3:24
2 Cor 5:21

1:31
†Jer 9:24
2 Cor 10:17

2:1
1 Cor 1:17

2:3
2 Cor 10:1
Gal 4:13

2:4
1 Cor 4:20

2:5
2 Cor 4:7; 6:7

2:6
Eph 4:13
Phil 3:15
Heb 5:14

2:7
Rom 16:25

2:8
Jas 2:1

²⁵This "foolish" plan of God is far wiser than the wisest of human plans, and God's weakness is far stronger than the greatest of human strength.

²⁶Remember, dear brothers and sisters, that few of you were wise in the world's eyes, or powerful, or wealthy when God called you. ²⁷Instead, God deliberately chose things the world considers foolish in order to shame those who think they are wise. And he chose those who are powerless to shame those who are powerful. ²⁸God chose things despised by the world, things counted as nothing at all, and used them to bring to nothing what the world considers important, ²⁹so that no one can ever boast in the presence of God.

³⁰God alone made it possible for you to be in Christ Jesus. For our benefit God made Christ to be wisdom itself. He is the one who made us acceptable to God. He made us pure and holy, and he gave himself to purchase our freedom. ³¹As the Scriptures say,

"The person who wishes to boast
    should boast only of what the Lord has done."*

Paul Preaches Wisdom

2 Dear brothers and sisters,* when I first came to you I didn't use lofty words and brilliant ideas to tell you God's message.* ²For I decided to concentrate only on Jesus Christ and his death on the cross. ³I came to you in weakness—timid and trembling. ⁴And my message and my preaching were very plain. I did not use wise and persuasive speeches, but the Holy Spirit was powerful among you. ⁵I did this so that you might trust the power of God rather than human wisdom.

⁶Yet when I am among mature Christians, I do speak with words of wisdom, but not the kind of wisdom that belongs to this world, and not the kind that appeals to the rulers of this world, who are being brought to nothing. ⁷No, the wisdom we speak of is the secret wisdom of God,* which was hidden in former times, though he made it for our benefit before the world began. ⁸But the rulers of this world have not understood it; if

1:31 Jer 9:24.   **2:1a** Greek *Brothers.*   **2:1b** Greek *mystery;* other manuscripts read *testimony.*   **2:7** Greek *we speak God's wisdom in a mystery.*

• **1:25** The message of Christ's death for sins sounds foolish to those who don't believe. Death seems to be the end of the road, the ultimate weakness. But Jesus did not stay dead. His resurrection demonstrated his power even over death. And he will save us from eternal death and give us everlasting life if we trust him as Savior and Lord. This sounds so simple that many people won't accept it. They try other ways to obtain eternal life (being good, being wise, etc.). But all their attempts are futile. The "foolish" people who simply accept Christ's offer are actually the wisest of all, because they alone will live eternally with God.

1:27 Is Christianity against rational thinking? Christians clearly do believe in using their minds to weigh the evidence and make wise choices. Paul is declaring that no amount of human knowledge can replace or bypass Christ's work on the cross. If it could, Christ would be accessible only to the intellectually gifted and well educated and not to ordinary people or to children.

1:28-31 Paul continues to emphasize that the way to receive salvation is so simple that *any* person who wants to can understand it. Skill and wisdom do not get a person into God's Kingdom—simple faith does. So no one can boast that personal achievements helped him or her secure eternal life. Salvation is totally from God through Jesus' death. There is *nothing* we can do to earn our salvation; we need only to accept what Jesus has already done for us.

1:30 God is our source and the reason for our personal relationship with Christ. Our union and identification with Christ results in our having God's wisdom (Colossians 2:3), being acceptable to God (2 Corinthians 5:21), being pure (1 Thessalonians 4:3-7), and having the penalty for our sins paid by Jesus (Mark 10:45).

2:1 Paul is referring to his first visit to Corinth during his second missionary journey (A.D. 51), when he founded the church (Acts 18:1ff).

2:1-5 A brilliant scholar, Paul could have overwhelmed his listeners with intellectual arguments. Instead, he shared the simple message of Jesus Christ by allowing the Holy Spirit to guide his words. In sharing the Good News with others, we should follow Paul's example and keep our message simple and basic. The Holy Spirit will give power to our words and use them to bring glory to Jesus.

• **2:4** Paul's confidence was not in his keen intellect or speaking ability but in his knowledge that the Holy Spirit was helping and guiding him. Paul is not denying the importance of study and preparation for preaching; he had a thorough education in the Scriptures. Effective preaching results from studious preparation and reliance on the work of the Holy Spirit. Don't use Paul's statement as an excuse for not studying or preparing.

• **2:7** God's "secret wisdom . . . which was hidden" was his offer of salvation to all people. Originally unknown to humanity, this plan became crystal clear when Jesus rose from the dead. His resurrection proved that he had power over sin and death and could offer us this power as well (see also 1 Peter 1:10-12 and the first note on Romans 16:25-27). God's plan, however, is still hidden to unbelievers because they either refuse to accept it, choose to ignore it, or simply haven't heard about it.

2:8 Jesus was misunderstood and rejected by those whom the world considered wise and great. He was put to death by the rulers in Palestine—the high priest, King Herod, Pilate, and the Pharisees and Sadducees. Jesus' rejection by these rulers had been predicted in Isaiah 53:3 and Zechariah 12:10, 11.

they had, they would never have crucified our glorious Lord. ⁹That is what the Scriptures mean when they say,

> "No eye has seen, no ear has heard,
>   and no mind has imagined
> what God has prepared
>   for those who love him."*

¹⁰But we know these things because God has revealed them to us by his Spirit, and his Spirit searches out everything and shows us even God's deep secrets. ¹¹No one can know what anyone else is really thinking except that person alone, and no one can know God's thoughts except God's own Spirit. ¹²And God has actually given us his Spirit (not the world's spirit) so we can know the wonderful things God has freely given us. ¹³When we tell you this, we do not use words of human wisdom. We speak words given to us by the Spirit, using the Spirit's words to explain spiritual truths.* ¹⁴But people who aren't Christians can't understand these truths from God's Spirit. It all sounds foolish to them because only those who have the Spirit can understand what the Spirit means. ¹⁵We who have the Spirit understand these things, but others can't understand us at all. ¹⁶How could they? For,

> "Who can know what the Lord is thinking?
>   Who can give him counsel?"*

But we can understand these things, for we have the mind of Christ.

Paul and Apollos, Servants of Christ

3 Dear brothers and sisters,* when I was with you I couldn't talk to you as I would to mature Christians. I had to talk as though you belonged to this world or as though you were infants in the Christian life.* ²I had to feed you with milk and not with solid food, because you couldn't handle anything stronger. And you still aren't ready, ³for you are still controlled by your own sinful desires. You are jealous of one another and quarrel with each other. Doesn't that prove you are controlled by your own desires? You are acting like people who don't belong to the Lord. ⁴When one of you says, "I am a follower of Paul," and another says, "I prefer Apollos," aren't you acting like those who are not Christians?*

2:9 †Isa 64:4; 65:17

2:10 Matt 11:25; 13:11 John 14:26; 15:26; 16:13-15 1 Jn 2:27

2:11 Prov 20:27 Jer 17:9 Rom 11:33

2:12 John 16:13-15 Rom 8:15 1 Cor 1:27

2:13 1 Cor 1:17; 2:4 2 Pet 1:20-21

2:14 John 8:47; 14:17 Jude 1:19

2:15 1 Cor 3:1 Gal 6:1 1 Jn 2:20

2:16 †Isa 40:13 Rom 11:34

3:1 Gal 6:1 Eph 4:14

3:2 John 16:2 Heb 5:12-13 1 Pet 2:2

3:3 Rom 13:13 1 Cor 1:10-11; 11:18

3:4 1 Cor 1:12

2:9 Isa 64:4.   **2:13** Or *explaining spiritual truths in spiritual language,* or *explaining spiritual truths to spiritual people.*
2:16 Isa 40:13.   **3:1a** Greek *Brothers.*   **3:1b** Greek *in Christ.*   **3:4** Greek *aren't you merely human?*

2:9 We cannot imagine all that God has in store for us, both in this life and for eternity. He will create a new heaven and a new earth (Isaiah 65:17; Revelation 21:1), and we will live with him forever. Until then, his Holy Spirit comforts and guides us. Knowing the wonderful and eternal future that awaits us gives us hope and courage to press on in this life, to endure hardship, and to avoid giving in to temptation. This world is not all there is. The best is yet to come.

• **2:10** "God's deep secrets" refers to God's unfathomable nature and his wonderful plan—Jesus' death and resurrection—and to the promise of salvation, revealed only to those who believe that what God says is true. Those who believe in Christ's death and resurrection and put their faith in him will know all they need to know to be saved. This knowledge, however, can't be grasped by even the wisest people unless they accept God's message. All who reject God's message are foolish, no matter how wise the world thinks they are.

2:13 Paul's words are authoritative because their source was the Holy Spirit. Paul was not merely giving his own personal views or his personal impression of what God had said. Under the inspiration of the Holy Spirit, he wrote the very thoughts and words of God.

• **2:14, 15** Non-Christians cannot understand spiritual truths, and they cannot grasp the concept that God's Spirit lives in believers. Don't expect most people to approve of or understand your decision to follow Christ. It all seems so silly to them. Just as a tone-deaf person cannot appreciate fine music, the person who rejects Christ cannot understand truths from God's Spirit. With the lines of communication broken, he or she won't be able to hear what God is saying to him or her.

2:15, 16 No one can know what the Lord is thinking (Romans 11:34), but through the guidance of the Holy Spirit, believers have insight into some of God's plans, thoughts, and actions. They, in fact, have "the mind of Christ." Through the Holy Spirit, we can begin to know God's thoughts, talk with him, and expect his answers to our prayers. Are you spending enough time with Christ to have his very mind in you? An intimate relationship with Christ comes only from spending time consistently in his presence and in his Word. Read Philippians 2:5ff for more on the mind of Christ.

3:1-3 Paul called the Corinthians infants in the Christian life because they were not yet spiritually healthy and mature. The proof was that they quarreled like children, allowing divisions to distract them. Immature Christians are "worldly," controlled by their own desires; mature believers are in tune with God's desires. How much influence do your desires have on your life? Your goal should be to let God's desires be yours. Being controlled by your own desires will stunt your growth.

3:5
Acts 18:24
Rom 12:3, 6
2 Cor 6:4

3:6
Acts 18:4-11

3:8
Pss 18:20; 62:12

3:9
Isa 61:3
Eph 2:20-22
1 Pet 2:5

3:10
Rom 15:20

3:11
Isa 28:16
Eph 2:20
1 Pet 2:4-6

3:13
1 Cor 4:5
2 Tim 1:12, 18; 4:8

3:15
Jude 1:23

3:16
1 Cor 6:19
2 Cor 6:16

3:17
Eph 2:21-22

3:18
Isa 5:21
1 Cor 8:2
Gal 6:3

3:19
†Job 5:13
1 Cor 1:20, 27

⁵Who is Apollos, and who is Paul, that we should be the cause of such quarrels? Why, we're only servants. Through us God caused you to believe. Each of us did the work the Lord gave us. ⁶My job was to plant the seed in your hearts, and Apollos watered it, but it was God, not we, who made it grow. ⁷The ones who do the planting or watering aren't important, but God is important because he is the one who makes the seed grow. ⁸The one who plants and the one who waters work as a team with the same purpose. Yet they will be rewarded individually, according to their own hard work. ⁹We work together as partners who belong to God. You are God's field, God's building—not ours.

¹⁰Because of God's special favor to me, I have laid the foundation like an expert builder. Now others are building on it. But whoever is building on this foundation must be very careful. ¹¹For no one can lay any other foundation than the one we already have—Jesus Christ. ¹²Now anyone who builds on that foundation may use gold, silver, jewels, wood, hay, or straw. ¹³But there is going to come a time of testing at the judgment day to see what kind of work each builder has done. Everyone's work will be put through the fire to see whether or not it keeps its value. ¹⁴If the work survives the fire, that builder will receive a reward. ¹⁵But if the work is burned up, the builder will suffer great loss. The builders themselves will be saved, but like someone escaping through a wall of flames.

¹⁶Don't you realize that all of you together are the temple of God and that the Spirit of God lives in* you? ¹⁷God will bring ruin upon anyone who ruins this temple. For God's temple is holy, and you Christians are that temple.

¹⁸Stop fooling yourselves. If you think you are wise by this world's standards, you will have to become a fool so you can become wise by God's standards. ¹⁹For the wisdom of this world is foolishness to God. As the Scriptures say,

"God catches those who think they are wise
    in their own cleverness."*

3:16 Or *among.*   **3:19** Job 5:13.

● **3:6** Paul planted the seed of the Good News message in people's hearts. He was a missionary pioneer; he brought the message of salvation. Apollos watered the seed. He helped the believers grow stronger in the faith. Paul founded the church in Corinth, and Apollos built on that foundation. Tragically, the believers in Corinth had split into factions, pledging loyalty to different teachers (see 1:11-13). After the preachers' work is completed, God is the one who makes Christians grow. Our leaders should certainly be respected, but we should never place them on pedestals that create barriers between people or set them up as a substitute for Christ.

3:7-9 God's work involves many different individuals with a variety of gifts and abilities. There are no superstars in this task, only team members performing their own special roles. We can become useful members of God's team by setting aside our desires to receive glory for what we do. Don't seek the praise that comes from people—it is comparatively worthless. Instead, seek approval from God.

● **3:10, 11** The foundation of the church—of all believers—is Jesus Christ. Paul laid this foundation (by preaching Christ) when he began the church at Corinth. Whoever builds the church—officers, teachers, preachers, parents, and others—must build with high-quality materials (right doctrine and right living, 3:12ff) that meet God's standards. Paul is not criticizing Apollos but challenging future church leaders to have sound preaching and teaching.

● **3:10-17** In the church built on Jesus Christ, each church member should be mature, spiritually sensitive, and doctrinally sound. However, the Corinthian church was filled with those whose work was "wood, hay, and straw," members who were immature, insensitive to one another, and vulnerable to wrong doctrine (3:1-4). No wonder they had so many problems. Local church members should be deeply committed to Christ. Can your Christian character stand the test?

3:11 A building is only as solid as its foundation. The foundation of our life is Jesus Christ; he is our base, our reason for being. Everything we are and do must fit into the pattern provided by him. Are you building your life on the only real and lasting foundation, or are you building on a faulty foundation, such as wealth, security, success, or fame?

● **3:13-15** Two sure ways to destroy a building are to tamper with the foundation and to build with inferior materials. The church must be built on Christ, not on any other person or principle. Christ will evaluate each minister's contribution to the life of the church, and judgment day will reveal the sincerity of each person's work. God will determine whether or not a person has been faithful to Jesus' instructions. Good work will be rewarded; unfaithful or inferior work will be discounted. "The builders themselves will be saved, but like someone escaping through a wall of flames" means that unfaithful workers will be saved, but only by the skin of their teeth. All their accomplishments will count for nothing.

3:16, 17 Just as our bodies are the "temple of the Holy Spirit" (6:19), the local church or Christian community is God's temple. Just as the Jews' Temple in Jerusalem was not to be destroyed, the church is not to be spoiled and ruined by divisions, controversy, or other sins as members come together to worship God.

3:18-21 Paul was not telling the Corinthian believers to neglect the pursuit of knowledge. He was warning them not to glory in the wisdom of this age. God's way of thinking is far above ours; he knows all the futile thoughts of the "wise." The Corinthians were boasting about the wisdom of their leaders and teachers. Their pride made them value the messenger more than the message. We are not to put our trust in anyone but God.

20And again,

"The Lord knows the thoughts of the wise,
    that they are worthless."*

21So don't take pride in following a particular leader. Everything belongs to you: 22Paul and Apollos and Peter*; the whole world and life and death; the present and the future. Everything belongs to you, 23and you belong to Christ, and Christ belongs to God.

Paul and the Corinthians

4 So look at Apollos and me as mere servants of Christ who have been put in charge of explaining God's secrets. 2Now, a person who is put in charge as a manager must be faithful. 3What about me? Have I been faithful? Well, it matters very little what you or anyone else thinks. I don't even trust my own judgment on this point. 4My conscience is clear, but that isn't what matters. It is the Lord himself who will examine me and decide.

5So be careful not to jump to conclusions before the Lord returns as to whether or not someone is faithful. When the Lord comes, he will bring our deepest secrets to light and will reveal our private motives. And then God will give to everyone whatever praise is due.

6Dear brothers and sisters,* I have used Apollos and myself to illustrate what I've been saying. If you pay attention to the Scriptures,* you won't brag about one of your leaders at the expense of another. 7What makes you better than anyone else? What do you have that God hasn't given you? And if all you have is from God, why boast as though you have accomplished something on your own?

8You think you already have everything you need! You are already rich! Without us you have become kings! I wish you really were on your thrones already, for then we would be reigning with you! 9But sometimes I think God has put us apostles on display, like prisoners of war at the end of a victor's parade, condemned to die. We have become a spectacle to the entire world—to people and angels alike.

10Our dedication to Christ makes us look like fools, but you are so wise! We are weak, but you are so powerful! You are well thought of, but we are laughed at. 11To this very hour we go hungry and thirsty, without enough clothes to keep us warm. We have endured many beatings, and we have no homes of our own. 12We have worked wearily with our own hands to earn our living. We bless those who curse us. We are patient with those who abuse us. 13We respond gently when evil things are said about us. Yet we are treated like the world's garbage, like everybody's trash—right up to the present moment.

14I am not writing these things to shame you, but to warn you as my beloved children.

3:20
†Ps 94:11

3:21
Rom 8:32

3:22
Rom 8:38

3:23
1 Cor 11:3

4:1
Rom 16:25
Titus 1:7

4:2
Luke 12:42

4:4
Ps 143:2

4:5
Matt 7:1
1 Cor 3:8
2 Cor 5:10
Rev 20:12

4:6
1 Cor 1:12, 31

4:7
John 3:27
Rom 12:3, 6

4:8
Rev 3:17, 21

4:9
Rom 8:36
Heb 10:33

4:10
1 Cor 1:18; 3:18
2 Cor 11:19

4:11
Acts 23:2
Rom 8:35
2 Cor 11:23-27

4:12
Matt 5:44
Acts 18:3
1 Pet 3:9

4:13
Lam 3:45

4:14
1 Cor 6:5; 15:34
2 Cor 6:13

3:20 Ps 94:11.   **3:22** Greek *Cephas*.   **4:6a** Greek *Brothers*.   **4:6b** Or *You must learn not to go beyond "what is written," so that.*

3:22 Paul says that both life and death are ours. While nonbelievers are victims of life, swept along by its current and wondering if there is meaning to it, believers can use life well because they understand its true purpose. Nonbelievers can only fear death. For believers, however, death holds no terrors because Christ has conquered all fears (see 1 John 4:18). Death is only the beginning of eternal life with God.

• **4:1, 2** Paul urged the Corinthians to think of him, Peter, and Apollos as mere servants of Christ entrusted with the secret things of God (see the note on 2:7). A servant does what his master tells him to do. We must do what God tells us to do in the Bible and through his Holy Spirit. Each day God presents us with needs and opportunities that challenge us to do what we know is right.

4:5 It is tempting to judge fellow Christians, evaluating whether or not they are good followers of Christ. But only God knows a person's heart, and he is the only one with the right to judge. Paul's warning to the Corinthians should also warn us. We are to confront those who are sinning (see 5:12, 13), but we must not judge who is a better servant for Christ. When you judge someone, you invariably consider yourself better—and that is arrogant.

• **4:6, 7** How easy it is for us to become attached to a spiritual leader. When someone has helped us, it's natural to feel loyalty. But Paul warns against having such pride in our favorite leaders that we cause divisions in the church. Any true spiritual leader is a representative of Christ and has nothing to offer that God hasn't given him or her. Don't let your loyalty cause strife, slander, or broken relationships. Make sure that your deepest loyalties are to Christ and not to his human agents. Those who spend more time in debating church leadership than in declaring Christ's message don't have the mind of Christ.

4:6-13 The Corinthians had split into various cliques, each following its favorite preacher (Paul, Apollos, Peter, etc.). Each clique really believed it was the only one to have the whole truth and thus felt spiritually proud. But Paul told the groups not to boast about being tied to a particular preacher, because each preacher was simply a humble servant who had suffered for the same message of salvation in Jesus Christ. No preacher of God has more status than another.

4:15
Gal 4:19

4:16
1 Cor 11:1
Phil 3:17
1 Thes 1:6

4:17
Acts 16:1; 19:22
1 Tim 1:2

4:19
Acts 18:21
1 Cor 16:5
2 Cor 1:15-16

4:20
1 Cor 2:4

4:21
2 Cor 1:23; 2:1

5:1
Lev 18:7-8
Deut 22:30; 27:20
Eph 5:3

5:3
Col 2:5

¹⁵For even if you had ten thousand others to teach you about Christ, you have only one spiritual father. For I became your father in Christ Jesus when I preached the Good News to you. ¹⁶So I ask you to follow my example and do as I do.

¹⁷That is the very reason I am sending Timothy—to help you do this. For he is my beloved and trustworthy child in the Lord. He will remind you of what I teach about Christ Jesus in all the churches wherever I go.

¹⁸I know that some of you have become arrogant, thinking I will never visit you again. ¹⁹But I will come—and soon—if the Lord will let me, and then I'll find out whether these arrogant people are just big talkers or whether they really have God's power. ²⁰For the Kingdom of God is not just fancy talk; it is living by God's power. ²¹Which do you choose? Should I come with punishment and scolding, or should I come with quiet love and gentleness?

2. Disorder in the church
Paul Condemns Spiritual Pride

5 I can hardly believe the report about the sexual immorality going on among you, something so evil that even the pagans don't do it. I am told that you have a man in your church who is living in sin with his father's wife. ²And you are so proud of yourselves! Why aren't you mourning in sorrow and shame? And why haven't you removed this man from your fellowship?

³Even though I am not there with you in person, I am with you in the Spirit.* Concerning

5:3 Or *in spirit.*

CHURCH DISCIPLINE
The church, at times, must exercise discipline toward members who have sinned. But church discipline must be handled carefully, straightforwardly, and lovingly.

Situations

Unintentional error and/or private sin

Public sin and/or those done flagrantly and arrogantly

Steps (Matthew 18:15–17)

1. Go to the brother or sister; show the fault to him or her in private.
2. If he/she does not listen, go with one or two witnesses.
3. If he/she refuses to listen, take the matter before the church.

After these steps have been carried out, the next steps are

1. Remove the one in error from the fellowship (1 Corinthians 5:2–13).
2. The church gives united disapproval, but forgiveness and comfort are in order if he/she chooses to repent (2 Corinthians 2:5–8).
3. Do not associate with the disobedient person; and if you must, speak to him/her as one who needs a warning (2 Thessalonians 3:14, 15).
4. After two warnings, reject the person from the fellowship (Titus 3:10).

• **4:15** Paul was calling attention to his special role as the Corinthians' spiritual father. In an attempt to unify the church, Paul appealed to his relationship with them. By *father,* he meant he was the church's founder. Because he started the church, he could be trusted to have its best interests at heart. Paul's tough words were motivated by love—like the love a good father has for his children (see also 1 Thessalonians 2:11).

4:16 Paul told the Corinthians to follow his example. He was able to make this statement because he walked close to God, spent time in God's Word and in prayer, and was aware of God's presence in his life at all times. God was Paul's example; therefore, Paul's life could be an example to other Christians. Paul wasn't expecting others to imitate everything he did, but they should imitate those aspects of his beliefs and conduct that were modeling Christ's way of living.

4:17 Timothy had traveled with Paul on Paul's second missionary journey (see Acts 16:1-3) and was a key person in the growth of the early church. Timothy probably did not deliver this letter to Corinth but more likely arrived there shortly after the letter came (see 16:10). Timothy's role was to see that Paul's advice was read and implemented. Then he was to return to Paul and report on the church's progress.

4:18-20 Some people talk a lot about faith, but that's all it is—

talk. They may know all the right words to say, but their lives don't reflect God's power. Paul says that the Kingdom of God is to be *lived,* not just discussed. There is a big difference between knowing the right words and living them out. Don't be content to have the right answers about Christ. Let your life show that God's power is really working in you.

4:19 It is not known whether Paul ever returned to Corinth, but it is likely. In 2 Corinthians 2:1, he writes that he decided not to make "another painful visit," implying that he had had a previous painful confrontation with the Corinthian believers (see 2 Corinthians 12:14; 13:1; and the note on 2 Corinthians 2:1).

• **5:1ff** The church must discipline flagrant sin among its members. Such sins left unchecked can polarize and paralyze a church. The correction, however, should never be vengeful. Instead, it should be given to help bring about a cure. The Corinthian believers had refused to deal with a specific sin in the church: A man was having an affair with his mother (or stepmother). The church was ignoring the situation, and Paul was saying that it had a responsibility to maintain the standards of morality found in God's commandments. God tells us not to judge others. But he also tells us not to tolerate flagrant sin because allowing such sin to go undisciplined will have a dangerous effect on other believers (5:6).

the one who has done this, I have already passed judgment ⁴in the name of the Lord Jesus. You are to call a meeting of the church,* and I will be there in spirit, and the power of the Lord Jesus will be with you as you meet. ⁵Then you must cast this man out of the church and into Satan's hands, so that his sinful nature will be destroyed* and he himself* will be saved when the Lord returns.

⁶How terrible that you should boast about your spirituality, and yet you let this sort of thing go on. Don't you realize that if even one person is allowed to go on sinning, soon all will be affected? ⁷Remove this wicked person from among you so that you can stay pure.* Christ, our Passover Lamb, has been sacrificed for us. ⁸So let us celebrate the festival, not by eating the old bread* of wickedness and evil, but by eating the new bread* of purity and truth.

⁹When I wrote to you before, I told you not to associate with people who indulge in sexual sin. ¹⁰But I wasn't talking about unbelievers who indulge in sexual sin, or who are greedy or are swindlers or idol worshipers. You would have to leave this world to avoid people like that. ¹¹What I meant was that you are not to associate with anyone who claims to be a Christian* yet indulges in sexual sin, or is greedy, or worships idols, or is abusive, or a drunkard, or a swindler. Don't even eat with such people.

¹²It isn't my responsibility to judge outsiders, but it certainly is your job to judge those inside the church who are sinning in these ways. ¹³God will judge those on the outside; but as the Scriptures say, "You must remove the evil person from among you."*

Avoiding Lawsuits with Christians

6 When you have something against another Christian, why do you file a lawsuit and ask a secular court to decide the matter, instead of taking it to other Christians to decide who is right? ²Don't you know that someday we Christians are going to judge the world?

5:4 Or *In the name of the Lord Jesus, you are to call a meeting of the church.*   **5:5a** Or *so that he will die;* Greek reads *for the destruction of the flesh.*   **5:5b** Greek *and the spirit.*   **5:6-7** Greek *Don't you realize that even a little leaven spreads quickly through the whole batch of dough? ⁷Purge out the old leaven so that you can be a new batch of dough, just as you are already unleavened.*   **5:8a** Greek *not with old leaven.*   **5:8b** Greek *but with unleavened [bread].*   **5:11** Greek *a brother.*   **5:13** Deut 17:7.

Margin references:

5:4 2 Thes 3:6
5:5 1 Tim 1:20
5:6 Matt 16:6, 12; Gal 5:9
5:7 Exod 12:3-6, 21; Isa 53:7; 1 Pet 1:19; Rev 5:6
5:8 Exod 12:15-19; Deut 16:3
5:9 2 Cor 6:14
5:10 John 17:15
5:11 Rom 16:17; 2 Thes 3:6; 2 Jn 1:10
5:12 Mark 4:11
5:13 †Deut 17:7; 19:19; 21:21, 24; 24:7
6:1 Matt 18:17
6:2 Dan 7:22; Luke 22:30; Rev 3:21

• **5:5** To cast this man "into Satan's hands" means to exclude him from the fellowship of believers. Without the spiritual support of Christians, this man would be left alone with his sin and Satan, and perhaps this would drive him to repentance. "So that his sinful nature will be destroyed" states the hope that the experience would bring him to God to destroy his sinful nature through his turning from sin. *Sinful nature* could mean his body or flesh. This alternative translation would imply that Satan would afflict him physically and thus bring him to God. Putting someone out of the church should be a last resort in disciplinary action. It should not be done out of vengeance but out of love, just as parents punish children to correct and restore them. The church's role should be to help, not hurt, offenders, motivating them to repent of their sins and to return to the fellowship of the church.

• **5:6** Paul was writing to those who wanted to ignore this church problem. They didn't realize that allowing public sin to exist in the church affects all its members. Paul does not expect anyone to be sinless—all believers struggle with sin daily. Instead, he is speaking against those who deliberately sin, feel no guilt, and refuse to repent. This kind of sin cannot be tolerated in the church because it affects others. We have a responsibility to other believers. Blatant sins, left uncorrected, confuse and divide the congregation. While believers should encourage, pray for, and build up one another, they must also be intolerant of sin that jeopardizes the spiritual health of the church.

5:7, 8 As the Hebrews prepared for their exodus from slavery in Egypt, they were commanded to prepare bread without yeast because they didn't have time to wait for it to rise. And because yeast also was a symbol of sin, they were commanded to sweep all of it out of the house (Exodus 12:15; 13:7). Christ is our Passover lamb, the perfect sacrifice for our sin. Because he has delivered us from the slavery of sin, we should have nothing to do with the sins of the past ("old bread").

5:9 Paul is referring to an earlier letter to the Corinthian church, often called the lost letter because it has not been preserved.

• **5:10, 11** Paul makes it clear that we should not disassociate ourselves from unbelievers—otherwise we could not carry out Christ's command to tell them about salvation (Matthew 28:18-20). But we are to distance ourselves from the person who claims to be a Christian, yet indulges in sins explicitly forbidden in Scripture by rationalizing his or her actions. By rationalizing sin, a person harms others for whom Christ died and dims the image of God in himself or herself. A church that includes such a person is hardly fit to be the light of the world. To do so would distort the picture of Christ it presents to the world. Church leaders must be ready to correct, in love, for the sake of spiritual unity.

• **5:12** The Bible consistently tells us not to criticize people by gossiping or making rash judgments. At the same time, however, we are to judge and deal with sin that can hurt others. Paul's instructions should not be used to handle trivial matters or to take revenge; nor should they be applied to individual problems between believers. These verses are instructions for dealing with open sin in the church by a person who claims to be a Christian and yet who sins without remorse. The church is to confront and discipline such a person in love. Also see the notes on 4:5 and 5:1ff.

• **6:1-6** In chapter 5, Paul explained what to do with open immorality in the congregation. In chapter 6, he teaches how the congregation should handle smaller problems between believers. Society has set up a legal system in which disagreements can be resolved in courts. But Paul declares that Christians should not have to go to a secular court to resolve their differences. As Christians, we have the Holy Spirit and the mind of Christ, so why should we turn to those who lack God's wisdom? Because of all that we have been given as believers, and because of the authority that we will have in the future to judge the world and the angels, we should be

And since you are going to judge the world, can't you decide these little things among yourselves? ³Don't you realize that we Christians will judge angels? So you should surely be able to resolve ordinary disagreements here on earth. ⁴If you have legal disputes about such matters, why do you go to outside judges who are not respected by the church? ⁵I am saying this to shame you. Isn't there anyone in all the church who is wise enough to decide these arguments? ⁶But instead, one Christian* sues another—right in front of unbelievers!

⁷To have such lawsuits at all is a real defeat for you. Why not just accept the injustice and leave it at that? Why not let yourselves be cheated? ⁸But instead, you yourselves are the ones who do wrong and cheat even your own Christian brothers and sisters.*

Avoiding Sexual Sin

⁹Don't you know that those who do wrong will have no share in the Kingdom of God? Don't fool yourselves. Those who indulge in sexual sin, who are idol worshipers, adulterers, male prostitutes, homosexuals, ¹⁰thieves, greedy people, drunkards, abusers, and swindlers—none of these will have a share in the Kingdom of God. ¹¹There was a time when some of you were just like that, but now your sins have been washed away,* and you have been set apart for God. You have been made right with God because of what the Lord Jesus Christ and the Spirit of our God have done for you.

¹²You may say, "I am allowed to do anything." But I reply, "Not everything is good for you." And even though "I am allowed to do anything," I must not become a slave to anything. ¹³You say, "Food is for the stomach, and the stomach is for food." This is true,

6:6 Greek *one brother.*   **6:8** Greek *brothers.*   **6:11** Or *you have been cleansed.*

6:3
2 Pet 2:4
Jude 1:6

6:5
1 Cor 4:14

6:7
Matt 5:39
1 Thes 5:15
1 Pet 3:9

6:8
1 Thes 4:6

6:9-10
Gal 5:19-21
Eph 5:5
Rev 22:15

6:11
Acts 22:16
Rom 8:30
1 Cor 1:2, 30

6:12
1 Cor 10:23

6:13
Col 2:22
1 Thes 4:3-5

---

able to deal with disputes among ourselves. See John 5:22 and Revelation 3:21 for more on judging the world. Judging angels is mentioned in 2 Peter 2:4 and Jude 1:6.

6:6-8 Why did Paul say that Christians should not take their disagreements to unbelievers in secular courts? (1) If the judge and jury are not Christians, they are not likely to be sensitive to Christian values. (2) The basis for going to court is often revenge; this should never be a Christian's motive. (3) Lawsuits harm the cause of Christ and make the church look bad, causing unbelievers to focus on its problems rather than on its purpose.

6:9-11 Paul is describing characteristics of unbelievers. He doesn't mean that all those who have indulged in sexual sin or who have been idol worshipers, adulterers, male prostitutes, homosexuals, thieves, greedy people, drunkards, abusers, and swindlers are automatically and irrevocably excluded from heaven. Christians come out of all kinds of different backgrounds, including these. They may still struggle with evil desires, but they should not continue in these practices. In 6:11, Paul clearly states that even those who sin in these ways can have their lives changed by Christ. However, those who say that they are Christians but persist in these practices with no sign of remorse will not inherit the Kingdom of God. Such people need to reevaluate their lives to see if they truly believe in Christ.

• **6:9-11** In a permissive society it is easy for Christians to overlook or tolerate some immoral behavior (greed, drunkenness, etc.) while remaining outraged at others (homosexuality, thievery). We must not participate in sin or condone it in any way; we cannot be selective about what we condemn or excuse. Staying away from more "acceptable" forms of sin is difficult, but it is no harder for us than it was for the Corinthians. God expects his followers in any age to have high standards.

6:11 Paul emphasizes God's action in making believers new people. The three aspects of God's work are all part of our salvation: Our sins were washed away, we were set apart for special use (sanctified), and we have been made right with God (justified).

6:12 Apparently the church had been quoting and misapplying the words "I am allowed to do anything." Some Christians in Corinth were excusing their sins by saying that (1) Christ had taken away all sin, and so they had complete freedom to live as they pleased, or (2) what they were doing was not strictly forbidden by Scripture. Paul answered both these excuses: (1) While Christ has

taken away our sin, this does not give us freedom to go on doing what we know is wrong. The New Testament specifically forbids many sins (see 6:9, 10) that were originally prohibited in the Old Testament (see Romans 12:9-21; 13:8-10). (2) Some actions are not sinful in themselves, but they are not appropriate because they can control our life and lead us away from God. (3) Some actions may hurt others. Anything we do that hurts rather than helps others is not right.

6:12, 13 Many of the world's religions teach that the soul or spirit is important but the body is not; and Christianity has sometimes been influenced by these ideas. In truth, however, Christianity takes very seriously the realm of the physical. We worship a God who created a physical world and pronounced it good. He promises us a new earth, where real people will have transformed physical lives—not a pink cloud where disembodied souls listen to harp music. At the heart of Christianity is the story of God himself taking on flesh and blood and coming to live with us, offering both physical healing and spiritual restoration.

We humans, like Adam, are a combination of dust and spirit. Just as our spirits affect our bodies, so our physical bodies affect our spirits. We cannot commit sin with our bodies without damaging our souls because our bodies and souls are inseparably joined. In the new earth we will have resurrection bodies that are not corrupted by sin. Then we will enjoy the fullness of our salvation.

• **6:12, 13** Freedom is a mark of the Christian faith—freedom from sin and guilt, and freedom to use and enjoy anything that comes from God. But Christians should not abuse this freedom and hurt themselves or others. Drinking too much leads to alcoholism; gluttony leads to obesity. Be careful that what God has allowed you to enjoy doesn't grow into a bad habit that controls you. For more about Christian freedom and everyday behavior, read chapter 8.

• **6:13** Sexual immorality is a temptation that is always before us. In movies and on television, sex outside marriage is treated as a normal, even desirable, part of life, while marriage is often shown as confining and joyless. We can even be looked down on by others if we are suspected of being pure. But God does not forbid sexual sin just to be difficult. He knows its power to destroy us physically and spiritually. No one should underestimate the power of sexual immorality. It has devastated countless lives and destroyed families, churches, communities, and even nations. God wants to protect us from damaging ourselves and others, and so he offers to fill us—our loneliness, our desires—with himself.

though someday God will do away with both of them. But our bodies were not made for sexual immorality. They were made for the Lord, and the Lord cares about our bodies. ¹⁴And God will raise our bodies from the dead by his marvelous power, just as he raised our Lord from the dead. ¹⁵Don't you realize that your bodies are actually parts of Christ? Should a man take his body, which belongs to Christ, and join it to a prostitute? Never! ¹⁶And don't you know that if a man joins himself to a prostitute, he becomes one body with her? For the Scriptures say, "The two are united into one."* ¹⁷But the person who is joined to the Lord becomes one spirit with him.

¹⁸Run away from sexual sin! No other sin so clearly affects the body as this one does. For sexual immorality is a sin against your own body. ¹⁹Or don't you know that your body is the temple of the Holy Spirit, who lives in you and was given to you by God? You do not belong to yourself, ²⁰for God bought you with a high price. So you must honor God with your body.

6:14
Acts 2:24
Rom 6:5
1 Cor 15:15, 20
Eph 1:19-20

6:17
John 17:21-23
Rom 8:9-11, 16
2 Cor 3:17
Gal 2:20

6:18
1 Thes 4:3-4

6:19
Rom 14:7-8
1 Cor 3:16
2 Cor 6:16

6:20
Phil 1:20
1 Pet 1:18-19

B. PAUL ANSWERS CHURCH QUESTIONS (7:1—16:24)

After discussing disorder in the church, Paul moves to the list of questions that the Corinthians had sent him, including subjects of marriage, singleness, eating meat offered to idols, propriety in worship, orderliness in the Lord's Supper, spiritual gifts, and the resurrection. Questions that plague churches today are remarkably similar to these, so we can receive specific guidance in these areas from this letter.

1. Instruction on Christian marriage

7 Now about the questions you asked in your letter. Yes, it is good to live a celibate life. ²But because there is so much sexual immorality, each man should have his own wife, and each woman should have her own husband.

³The husband should not deprive his wife of sexual intimacy, which is her right as a married woman, nor should the wife deprive her husband. ⁴The wife gives authority over

7:1
1 Cor 7:8, 26

7:3
Exod 21:10
1 Pet 3:7

6:16 Gen 2:24.

6:15-17 This teaching about sexual immorality and prostitutes was especially important for the Corinthian church because the temple of the love goddess Aphrodite was in Corinth. This temple employed more than a thousand prostitutes as priestesses, and sex was part of the worship ritual. Paul clearly stated that Christians are to have no part in sexual immorality, even if it is acceptable and popular in our culture.

6:18 Christians are free to be all they can be for God, but they are not free *from* God. God created sex to be a beautiful and essential ingredient of marriage, but sexual sin—sex outside the marriage relationship—*always* hurts someone. It hurts God because it shows that we prefer following our own desires instead of the leading of the Holy Spirit. It hurts others because it violates the commitment so necessary to a relationship. It often brings disease to our bodies. And it deeply affects our personality, which responds in anguish when we harm ourselves physically and spiritually.

• **6:19, 20** What did Paul mean when he said that our body belongs to God? Many people say they have the right to do whatever they want with their own bodies. Although they think that this is freedom, they are really enslaved to their own desires. When we become Christians, the Holy Spirit comes to live in us. Therefore, we no longer own our bodies. That God bought us "with a high price" refers to slaves purchased at an auction. Christ's death freed us from sin but also obligates us to his service. If you live in a building owned by someone else, you try not to violate the building's rules. Because your body belongs to God, you must not violate his standards for living.

7:1 The Corinthians had written to Paul, asking him several questions relating to the Christian life and problems in the church. The first question was whether it was good to be married. Paul answers this and other questions in the remainder of this letter.

7:1ff Christians in Corinth were surrounded by sexual temptation. The city had a reputation even among pagans for sexual immorality and religious prostitution. It was to this kind of society that Paul delivered these instructions on sex and marriage. The Corinthians needed special, specific instructions because of their culture's immoral standards. For more on Paul's teaching about marriage, see Ephesians 5.

7:3-5 Sexual temptations are difficult to withstand because they appeal to the normal and natural desires that God has given us. Marriage provides God's way to satisfy these natural sexual desires and to strengthen the partners against temptation. Married couples have the responsibility to care for each other; therefore, husbands and wives should not withhold themselves sexually from one another but should fulfill each other's needs and desires. (See also the note on 10:13.)

• **7:3-11** The Corinthian church was in turmoil because of the immorality of the culture around them. Some Greeks, in rejecting immorality, rejected sex and marriage altogether. The Corinthian Christians wondered if this was what they should do also, so they asked Paul several questions: "Because sex is perverted, shouldn't we also abstain in marriage?" "If my spouse is unsaved, should I seek a divorce?" "Should unmarried people and widows remain unmarried?" Paul answered many of these questions by saying, "For now, stay put. Be content in the situation where God has placed you. If you're married, don't seek to be single. If you're single, don't seek to be married. Live God's way, one day at a time, and he will show you what to do."

• **7:4** Spiritually, our bodies belong to God when we become Christians because Jesus Christ bought us by paying the price to release us from sin (see 6:19, 20). Physically, our bodies belong to our spouses because God designed marriage so that, through the union of husband and wife, the two become one (Genesis 2:24). Paul stressed complete equality in sexual relationships. Neither male nor female should seek dominance or autonomy.

7:5
1 Thes 3:5

her body to her husband, and the husband also gives authority over his body to his wife. ⁵So do not deprive each other of sexual relations. The only exception to this rule would be the agreement of both husband and wife to refrain from sexual intimacy for a limited time, so they can give themselves more completely to prayer. Afterward they should come together again so that Satan won't be able to tempt them because of their lack of self-control. ⁶This is only my suggestion. It's not meant to be an absolute rule. ⁷I wish everyone could get along without marrying, just as I do. But we are not all the same. God gives some the gift of marriage, and to others he gives the gift of singleness.

7:6
2 Cor 8:8

7:7
Matt 19:11-12
1 Cor 9:5; 12:11

7:9
1 Tim 5:14

⁸Now I say to those who aren't married and to widows—it's better to stay unmarried, just as I am. ⁹But if they can't control themselves, they should go ahead and marry. It's better to marry than to burn with lust.

7:10
Mal 2:14-16
Matt 5:32; 19:9
Mark 10:10-12
Luke 16:18

¹⁰Now, for those who are married I have a command that comes not from me, but from the Lord.* A wife must not leave her husband. ¹¹But if she does leave him, let her remain single or else go back to him. And the husband must not leave his wife.

7:12
2 Cor 11:17

¹²Now, I will speak to the rest of you, though I do not have a direct command from the Lord. If a Christian man* has a wife who is an unbeliever and she is willing to continue living with him, he must not leave her. ¹³And if a Christian woman has a husband who is an unbeliever, and he is willing to continue living with her, she must not leave him. ¹⁴For the Christian wife brings holiness to her marriage, and the Christian husband brings holiness to his marriage. Otherwise, your children would not have a godly influence, but now they are set apart for him. ¹⁵(But if the husband or wife who isn't a Christian insists on leaving, let them go. In such cases the Christian husband or wife is not required to stay with them, for God wants his children to live in peace.) ¹⁶You wives must remember that your husbands might be converted because of you. And you husbands must remember that your wives might be converted because of you.

7:14
Mal 2:15

7:15
Rom 14:19

7:16
Rom 11:14
1 Pet 3:1

7:17
1 Cor 4:17; 14:33

¹⁷You must accept whatever situation the Lord has put you in, and continue on as you

7:10 See Matt 5:32; 19:9; Mark 10:11-12; Luke 16:18.   **7:12** Greek *a brother.*

• **7:7** Both marriage and singleness are gifts from God. One is no morally better than the other, and both are valuable to accomplishing God's purposes. It is important for us, therefore, to accept our present situation. When Paul said he wished that all people were like him (unmarried), he was expressing his desire that more people would devote themselves *completely* to the ministry without the added concerns of a spouse and family, as he had done. He was not criticizing marriage—after all, it is God's created way of providing companionship and populating the earth.

7:9 Sexual pressure is not the best motive for getting married, but it is better to marry the right person than to "burn with lust." Many new believers in Corinth thought that all sex was wrong, and so engaged couples were deciding not to get married. In this passage, Paul was telling couples who wanted to marry that they should not frustrate their normal sexual drives by avoiding marriage. This does not mean, however, that people who have trouble controlling themselves should marry the first person who comes along. It is better to deal with the pressure of desire than to deal with an unhappy marriage.

7:12 Paul's "command" about the permanence of marriage (7:10) comes from the Old Testament (Genesis 2:24) and from Jesus (Mark 10:2-12). His *suggestion* in this verse is based on God's command, and Paul applies it to the situation the Corinthians were facing. Paul ranked the command above the suggestion because one is an eternal principle while the other is a specific application. Nevertheless, for people in similar situations, Paul's suggestion is the best advice they will get. Paul was a man of God, an apostle, and he had the mind of Christ.

• **7:12-14** Because of their desire to serve Christ, some people in the Corinthian church thought they ought to divorce their pagan spouses and marry Christians. But Paul affirmed the marriage commitment. God's ideal is for husbands and wives to stay together—even when one spouse is not a believer. The Christian

spouse should try to win the other to Christ. It would be easy to rationalize leaving; however, Paul makes a strong case for staying with the unbelieving spouse and being a positive influence on the marriage. Paul, like Jesus, believed that marriage is permanent (see Mark 10:1-9).

7:14 The blessings that flow to believers don't stop there but extend to others. God regards the marriage as set apart for his use by the presence of one Christian spouse. The other does not receive salvation automatically but is blessed by this relationship. The children of such a marriage have a godly influence and are set apart (because of God's blessing on the family unit) until they are old enough to make their own decision for Christ.

7:15, 16 This verse is misused by some as a loophole to get out of marriage. But Paul's statements were given to encourage the Christian spouse to try to get along with the unbeliever and make the marriage work. If, however, the unbelieving spouse insists on leaving, Paul said to let him or her go. The only alternative would be for the Christian to deny his or her faith to preserve the marriage, and that would be worse than dissolving the marriage. Paul's chief purpose in writing this was to urge the married couples to seek unity, not separation (see 7:17; 1 Peter 3:1, 2).

7:17 Apparently the Corinthians were ready to make wholesale changes without thinking through the ramifications. Paul was writing to say that people should be Christians where they are. You can do God's work and demonstrate your faith *anywhere*. If you became a Christian after marriage, and your spouse is not a believer, remember that you don't have to be married to a Christian to live for Christ. Don't assume that you are in the wrong place or stuck with the wrong person. You may be just where God wants you (see 7:20).

were when God first called you. This is my rule for all the churches. ¹⁸For instance, a man who was circumcised before he became a believer should not try to reverse it. And the man who was uncircumcised when he became a believer should not be circumcised now. ¹⁹For it makes no difference whether or not a man has been circumcised. The important thing is to keep God's commandments.

⁷:¹⁸
Acts 15:1-19
Gal 5:2

⁷:¹⁹
Rom 2:25-27
Gal 5:6; 6:15
Col 3:11

²⁰You should continue on as you were when God called you. ²¹Are you a slave? Don't let that worry you—but if you get a chance to be free, take it. ²²And remember, if you were a slave when the Lord called you, the Lord has now set you free from the awful power of sin. And if you were free when the Lord called you, you are now a slave of Christ. ²³God purchased you at a high price. Don't be enslaved by the world.* ²⁴So, dear brothers and sisters,* whatever situation you were in when you became a believer, stay there in your new relationship with God.

⁷:²²
John 8:36
Eph 6:6
1 Pet 2:16

⁷:²³
1 Cor 6:20
1 Pet 1:18

²⁵Now, about the young women who are not yet married. I do not have a command from the Lord for them. But the Lord in his kindness has given me wisdom that can be trusted, and I will share it with you. ²⁶Because of the present crisis,* I think it is best to remain just as you are. ²⁷If you have a wife, do not end the marriage. If you do not have a wife, do not get married. ²⁸But if you do get married, it is not a sin. And if a young woman gets married, it is not a sin. However, I am trying to spare you the extra problems that come with marriage.

⁷:²⁵
2 Cor 4:1
1 Tim 1:12-13

²⁹Now let me say this, dear brothers and sisters: The time that remains is very short, so husbands should not let marriage be their major concern. ³⁰Happiness or sadness or wealth should not keep anyone from doing God's work. ³¹Those in frequent contact with the things of the world should make good use of them without becoming attached to them, for this world and all it contains will pass away. ³²In everything you do, I want you to be free from the concerns of this life. An unmarried man can spend his time doing the Lord's work and thinking how to please him. ³³But a married man can't do that so well. He has to think about his earthly responsibilities and how to please his wife. ³⁴His interests are divided. In the same way, a woman who is no longer married or has never been married can be more devoted to the Lord in body and in spirit, while the married woman must be concerned about her earthly responsibilities and how to please her husband.

⁷:²⁹
Rom 13:11

⁷:³¹
1 Jn 2:17

⁷:³⁴
1 Tim 5:5

7:23 Greek *don't become slaves of people.* **7:24** Greek *brothers;* also in 7:29. **7:26** Or *pressures of life.*

7:18, 19 The ceremony of circumcision was an important part of the Jews' relationship with God. In fact, before Christ came, circumcision was commanded by God for those who claimed to follow him (Genesis 17:9-14). But after Christ's death, circumcision was no longer necessary (Acts 15; Romans 4:9-11; Galatians 5:2-4; Colossians 2:11). Pleasing God and obeying him are more important than observing traditional ceremonies.

• **7:20** We may become so concerned about what we *could* be doing for God somewhere else that we miss great opportunities right where we are. Paul says that when you become a Christian, you should continue on with the work you have previously been doing—provided it isn't immoral or unethical. Every job can become Christian work when you realize that it can be an opportunity to honor, serve, and speak out for Christ. Because God has placed you where you are, take advantage of every opportunity to serve him there.

7:22 Slavery was common throughout the Roman Empire. Some Christians in the Corinthian church were undoubtedly slaves. Paul said that although they were slaves to other human beings, they were free from the power of sin in their lives. People today are slaves to sin until they commit their lives to Christ, who alone can conquer sin's power. Sin, pride, and fear no longer have any claim over us, just as a slave owner no longer has power over the slaves he has sold. The Bible says we become Christ's slaves when we become Christians (Romans 6:18), but this actually means we gain our freedom, because sin no longer controls us.

7:26 Paul probably foresaw the impending persecution that the Roman government would soon bring upon Christians. He gave this practical advice because being unmarried would mean less suffering and more freedom to throw one's life into the cause of

Christ (7:29), even to the point of fearlessly dying for him. Paul's advice reveals his single-minded devotion to spreading the Good News.

• **7:28** Many people naively think that marriage will solve all their problems. Here are some problems marriage won't solve: (1) loneliness, (2) sexual temptation, (3) one's deepest emotional needs, (4) life's difficulties. Marriage alone does not hold two people together but commitment does—commitment to Christ and to each other despite conflicts and problems. As wonderful as it is, marriage does not automatically solve every problem. Whether married or single, we must be content with our situation and focus on Christ, not on loved ones, to help address our problems.

7:29 Paul urges all believers to make the most of their time before Christ's return. Every person in every generation should have this sense of urgency about telling the Good News to others. Life is short—there's not much time!

7:29-31 Paul urges believers not to regard marriage, home, or financial security as the ultimate goals of life. As much as possible, we should live unhindered by the cares of this world, not getting involved with burdensome mortgages, budgets, investments, or debts that might keep us from doing God's work. A married man or woman, as Paul points out (7:33, 34), must take care of earthly responsibilities but make every effort to keep them modest and manageable.

7:32-34 Some single people feel tremendous pressure to be married. They think their lives can be complete only with a spouse. But Paul underlines one advantage of being single—the potential of a greater focus on Christ and his work. If you are unmarried, use your special opportunity to serve Christ wholeheartedly.

35I am saying this for your benefit, not to place restrictions on you. I want you to do whatever will help you serve the Lord best, with as few distractions as possible. 36But if a man thinks he ought to marry his fiancée because he has trouble controlling his passions and time is passing, it is all right; it is not a sin. Let them marry. 37But if he has decided firmly not to marry and there is no urgency and he can control his passion, he does well not to marry. 38So the person who marries does well, and the person who doesn't marry does even better.

39A wife is married to her husband as long as he lives. If her husband dies, she is free to marry whomever she wishes, but this must be a marriage acceptable to the Lord.* 40But in my opinion it will be better for her if she doesn't marry again, and I think I am giving you counsel from God's Spirit when I say this.

2. Instruction on Christian freedom

Food Sacrificed to Idols

8 Now let's talk about food that has been sacrificed to idols. You think that everyone should agree with your perfect knowledge. While knowledge may make us feel important, it is love that really builds up the church. 2Anyone who claims to know all the answers doesn't really know very much. 3But the person who loves God is the one God knows and cares for.

4So now, what about it? Should we eat meat that has been sacrificed to idols? Well, we all know that an idol is not really a god and that there is only one God and no other. 5According to some people, there are many so-called gods and many lords, both in heaven and on earth. 6But we know that there is only one God, the Father, who created

7:39 Or *but only to a Christian;* Greek reads *but only in the Lord.*

7:38
Heb 13:4

7:39
Rom 7:2
2 Cor 6:14

7:40
1 Cor 7:6, 25

8:1
Acts 15:20, 29

8:2
1 Cor 3:18; 13:8-9
Gal 6:3

8:4
Deut 4:35, 39; 6:4
1 Cor 10:19

8:6
John 1:3
Acts 17:28
1 Cor 12:5
Eph 4:5-6
Col 1:16

STRONGER, WEAKER BELIEVERS

	Advice to
Stronger believer	Don't be proud of your maturity; don't flaunt your freedom. Act in love so you do not cause a weaker believer to stumble.
Weaker believer	Although you may not feel the same freedom in some areas as in others, take your time, pray to God, but do not force others to adhere to your stipulations. You would hinder other believers by making up rules and standards for how everyone ought to behave. Make sure your convictions are based on God's Word and are not simply an expression of your opinions.
Pastors and leaders	Teach correctly from God's Word, helping Christians to understand what is right and wrong in God's eyes and to see that they can have varied opinions on other issues and still be unified. Don't allow potential problems to get out of hand, causing splits and divisions.

Paul advises those who are more mature in the faith about how they must care about their brothers and sisters in Christ who have more tender consciences; those "weaker" brothers and sisters are advised concerning their growth; and pastors and leaders are instructed on how to deal with the conflicts that easily could arise between these groups.

7:38 When Paul says the unmarried person does even better, he is talking about the potential time available for service to God. The single person does not have the responsibility of caring for a spouse and raising a family. Singleness, however, does not ensure service to God; involvement in service depends on the commitment of the individual.

7:40 Paul's advice comes from the Holy Spirit, who guides and equips both single and married people to fulfill their roles.

• **8:1** Meat bought in the marketplace was likely to have been offered to an idol in one of the many pagan temples. Animals were brought to a temple, killed before an idol as part of a pagan religious ceremony, and eaten at a feast in the pagan temple or taken to butchers who sold the meat in the marketplace. The believers wondered if, by eating such meat, they were somehow participating in the worship of idols.

8:1-3 Love is more important than knowledge. Knowledge can make us look good and feel important, but we can all too easily

develop an arrogant, know-it-all attitude. Many people with strong opinions are unwilling to listen to and learn from God and others. We can obtain God's knowledge only by loving him (see James 3:17, 18). And we can know and be known by God only when we model him by showing love (1 John 4:7, 8).

• **8:4-9** Paul addressed these words to believers who weren't bothered by eating meat that had been offered to idols. Although idols were phony, and the pagan ritual of sacrificing to them was meaningless, eating such meat offended some Christians with sensitive consciences. Paul said, therefore, that mature believers should avoid eating meat offered to idols if it would violate the conscience of weak Christian.

everything, and we exist for him. And there is only one Lord, Jesus Christ, through whom God made everything and through whom we have been given life.

⁷However, not all Christians realize this. Some are accustomed to thinking of idols as being real, so when they eat food that has been offered to idols, they think of it as the worship of real gods, and their weak consciences are violated. ⁸It's true that we can't win God's approval by what we eat. We don't miss out on anything if we don't eat it, and we don't gain anything if we do. ⁹But you must be careful with this freedom of yours. Do not cause a brother or sister with a weaker conscience to stumble.

¹⁰You see, this is what can happen: Weak Christians who think it is wrong to eat this food will see you eating in the temple of an idol. You know there's nothing wrong with it, but they will be encouraged to violate their conscience by eating food that has been dedicated to the idol. ¹¹So because of your superior knowledge, a weak Christian,* for whom Christ died, will be destroyed. ¹²And you are sinning against Christ when you sin against other Christians* by encouraging them to do something they believe is wrong. ¹³If what I eat is going to make another Christian sin, I will never eat meat again as long as I live—for I don't want to make another Christian stumble.

Paul Gives Up His Rights

9 Do I not have as much freedom as anyone else?* Am I not an apostle? Haven't I seen Jesus our Lord with my own eyes? Isn't it because of my hard work that you are in the Lord? ²Even if others think I am not an apostle, I certainly am to you, for you are living proof that I am the Lord's apostle.

³This is my answer to those who question my authority as an apostle.* ⁴Don't we have the right to live in your homes and share your meals? ⁵Don't we have the right to bring a Christian wife* along with us as the other disciples and the Lord's brothers and Peter* do? ⁶Or is it only Barnabas and I who have to work to support ourselves? ⁷What soldier has to pay his own expenses? And have you ever heard of a farmer who harvests his crop and doesn't have the right to eat some of it? What shepherd takes care of a flock of sheep and isn't allowed to drink some of the milk? ⁸And this isn't merely human opinion. Doesn't God's law say the same thing? ⁹For the law of Moses says, "Do not keep an ox from eating as it treads out the grain."* Do you suppose God was thinking only about oxen when he said this? ¹⁰Wasn't he also speaking to us? Of course he was. Just as farm workers who plow fields and thresh the grain expect a share of the harvest, Christian workers should be paid by those they serve.

¹¹We have planted good spiritual seed among you. Is it too much to ask, in return, for mere food and clothing? ¹²If you support others who preach to you, shouldn't we have an even greater right to be supported? Yet we have never used this right. We would rather put up with anything than put an obstacle in the way of the Good News about Christ.

8:11 Greek *brother;* also in 8:13.   **8:12** Greek *brothers.*   **9:1** Greek *Am I not free?*   **9:3** Greek *those who examine me.*   **9:5a** Greek *a sister, a wife.*   **9:5b** Greek *Cephas.*   **9:9** Deut 25:4.

Cross-references (margin)

8:7 Rom 14:14; 1 Cor 10:18
8:8 Rom 14:17
8:9 Rom 14:1, 13, 21; 2 Cor 6:3; Gal 5:13
8:11 Rom 14:15, 20
8:12 Matt 18:6
8:13 Rom 14:21
9:1 Acts 9:3; 18:9; 1 Cor 15:8; 1 Tim 2:7; 2 Tim 1:11
9:2 2 Cor 3:2-3
9:4 Luke 10:8; 1 Cor 9:13-14
9:5 Matt 8:14; 12:46; Mark 6:2-3; Luke 6:15
9:6 2 Thes 3:8-9
9:7 Deut 20:6; Prov 27:18; 1 Cor 3:6, 8; 2 Tim 2:4
9:9 †Deut 25:4; 1 Tim 5:18
9:10 Rom 4:23-24; 2 Tim 2:6
9:11 Rom 15:27
9:12 2 Cor 6:3; 11:7-12

● 8:10-13 Christian freedom does not mean that anything goes. It means that our salvation is not obtained by good deeds or legalistic rules; it is the free gift of God (Ephesians 2:8, 9). Christian freedom, then, is inseparably tied to Christian responsibility. New believers are often very sensitive to what is right or wrong, what they should or shouldn't do. Some actions may be perfectly all right for us to do but may harm a Christian brother or sister who is still young in the faith and learning what the Christian life is all about. We must be careful not to offend a sensitive or younger Christian or, by our example, cause him or her to sin. When we love others, our freedom should be less important to us than strengthening the faith of a brother or sister in Christ.

9:1 Some Corinthians were questioning Paul's authority and rights as an apostle, so Paul gave his credentials: He actually saw and talked with the resurrected Christ, who called him to be an apostle (see Acts 9:3-18). Such credentials make the advice he gives in this letter more persuasive. In 2 Corinthians 10–13, Paul defends his apostleship in greater detail.

9:1 Changed lives were the evidence that God was using Paul. Does your faith have an impact on others? You can be a life-changer, helping others grow spiritually, if you dedicate yourself to being used by God and letting him make you effective.

● 9:4ff Paul uses himself as an illustration of giving up personal rights. Paul had the right to hospitality, to be married, and to be paid for his work. But he willingly gave up these rights to win people to Christ. When your focus is on living for Christ, your rights become comparatively unimportant.

9:4-10 Jesus said that workers deserve their wages (Luke 10:7). Paul echoes this thought and urges the church to be sure to pay their Christian workers. We have the responsibility to care for our pastors, teachers, and other spiritual leaders. It is our duty to see that those who serve us in the ministry are fairly and adequately compensated.

9:5 The Lord's brothers attained leadership status in the church at Jerusalem. James (one of Jesus' brothers), for example, led the way to an agreement at the Jerusalem council (Acts 15) and wrote the book of James.

9:13
Lev 6:16, 26
Num 18:8, 31

9:14
Matt 10:10
Luke 10:7
Gal 6:6
1 Tim 5:18

9:15
Acts 18:3
2 Cor 11:9-10

9:16
Acts 9:15
Rom 1:14

9:17
Gal 2:7
Eph 3:1-8
Phil 1:16, 17
Col 1:25

9:18
2 Cor 11:7; 12:13

9:19
Gal 5:13

9:20
Acts 16:3; 21:20-26
Rom 11:14

9:21
Rom 2:12, 14
Gal 6:2

¹³Don't you know that those who work in the Temple get their meals from the food brought to the Temple as offerings? And those who serve at the altar get a share of the sacrificial offerings. ¹⁴In the same way, the Lord gave orders that those who preach the Good News should be supported by those who benefit from it. ¹⁵Yet I have never used any of these rights. And I am not writing this to suggest that I would like to start now. In fact, I would rather die than lose my distinction of preaching without charge. ¹⁶For preaching the Good News is not something I can boast about. I am compelled by God to do it. How terrible for me if I didn't do it!

¹⁷If I were doing this of my own free will, then I would deserve payment. But God has chosen me and given me this sacred trust, and I have no choice. ¹⁸What then is my pay? It is the satisfaction I get from preaching the Good News without expense to anyone, never demanding my rights as a preacher.

¹⁹This means I am not bound to obey people just because they pay me, yet I have become a servant of everyone so that I can bring them to Christ. ²⁰When I am with the Jews, I become one of them so that I can bring them to Christ. When I am with those who follow the Jewish laws, I do the same, even though I am not subject to the law, so that I can bring them to Christ. ²¹When I am with the Gentiles who do not have the Jewish law,* I fit in with them as much as I can. In this way, I gain their confidence and bring them to Christ. But I do not discard the law of God; I obey the law of Christ.

²²When I am with those who are oppressed, I share their oppression so that I might bring

9:21 Greek *those without the law.*

WHY WE DON'T GIVE UP Perseverance, persistence, the prize!! The Christian life was never promised as an easy way to live; instead, Paul constantly reminds us that we must have a purpose and a plan because times will be difficult and Satan will attack. But we never persevere without the promise of a prize—a promise God will keep.	Reference	The Purpose	The Plan	The Prize
	1 Corinthians 9:24–27	• Run to get the prize • Run straight to the goal	• Practice strict self-control • Discipline your body, training it	• An eternal prize
	Galatians 6:7–10	• Don't get tired of doing good • Don't get discouraged and give up • Do good to everyone	• Live to please the Spirit	• Everlasting life
	Ephesians 6:10–20	• Put on all of God's armor • Pray on all occasions	• Use every piece of God's armor to resist the enemy	• Taking our stand against the Devil's strategies
	Philippians 3:12–14	• Keep working toward that day when you will be all that Christ Jesus saved me for	• Forget the past; strain to reach the end of the race	• The prize for which God calls us up to heaven
	2 Timothy 2:1–13	• Teach these great truths to people who are able to pass them on to others • Be strong in Christ's grace, even when your faith is faltering	• Endure suffering like a soldier, and don't get tied up in worldly affairs • Follow the Lord's rules, as an athlete must do in order to win • Work hard, like a farmer who enjoys the fruit of his labor	• We will live with Christ; we will reign with him • He remains faithful

---

9:13 As part of their pay, priests in the Temple would receive a portion of the offerings as their food (see Numbers 18:8-24).

9:16 Preaching the Good News was Paul's gift and calling, and he said he couldn't stop preaching even if he wanted to. Paul was driven by the desire to do what God wanted, using his gifts for God's glory. What special gifts has God given you? Are you motivated, like Paul, to honor God with your gifts?

9:19-27 In 9:19-22 Paul asserts that he has freedom to do anything; in 9:24-27 he emphasizes a life of strict discipline. The Christian life involves both freedom and discipline. The goals of Paul's life were to glorify God and bring people to Christ. Thus, he stayed free of any philosophical position or material entanglement that might sidetrack him, while he strictly disciplined him-

self to carry out his goal. For Paul, both freedom and discipline were important tools to be used in God's service.

9:22, 23 Paul gives several important principles for ministry: (1) Find common ground with those you contact; (2) avoid a know-it-all attitude; (3) make others feel accepted; (4) be sensitive to their needs and concerns; and (5) look for opportunities to tell them about Christ. These principles are just as valid for us as they were for Paul.

them to Christ. Yes, I try to find common ground with everyone so that I might bring them to Christ. ²³I do all this to spread the Good News, and in doing so I enjoy its blessings.

²⁴Remember that in a race everyone runs, but only one person gets the prize. You also must run in such a way that you will win. ²⁵All athletes practice strict self-control. They do it to win a prize that will fade away, but we do it for an eternal prize. ²⁶So I run straight to the goal with purpose in every step. I am not like a boxer who misses his punches.* ²⁷I discipline my body like an athlete, training it to do what it should. Otherwise, I fear that after preaching to others I myself might be disqualified.

Warnings against Idolatry

10 I don't want you to forget, dear brothers and sisters,* what happened to our ancestors in the wilderness long ago. God guided all of them by sending a cloud that moved along ahead of them, and he brought them all safely through the waters of the sea on dry ground. ²As followers of Moses, they were all baptized in the cloud and the sea. ³And all of them ate the same miraculous* food, ⁴and all of them drank the same miraculous water. For they all drank from the miraculous rock that traveled with them, and that rock was Christ. ⁵Yet after all this, God was not pleased with most of them, and he destroyed them in the wilderness.

⁶These events happened as a warning to us, so that we would not crave evil things as they did ⁷or worship idols as some of them did. For the Scriptures say, "The people celebrated with feasting and drinking, and they indulged themselves in pagan revelry."* ⁸And we must not engage in sexual immorality as some of them did, causing 23,000 of them to die in one day. ⁹Nor should we put Christ* to the test, as some of them did and then died from snakebites. ¹⁰And don't grumble as some of them did, for that is why God sent his angel of death to destroy them. ¹¹All these events happened to them as examples for us. They were written down to warn us, who live at the time when this age is drawing to a close.

¹²If you think you are standing strong, be careful, for you, too, may fall into the same sin. ¹³But remember that the temptations that come into your life are no different from

9:24
Phil 3:14
2 Tim 4:7

9:25
2 Tim 2:5; 4:8
1 Pet 5:4

9:26
1 Tim 6:12

9:27
Rom 8:13; 13:14
2 Cor 13:5

10:1
Exod 13:21-22;
14:15-22

10:3
Exod 16:4, 35
John 6:31-58

10:4
Exod 17:6
Num 20:11
John 6:31-58; 7:37

10:5
Num 14:16, 23

10:6
Num 11:4, 34
Ps 106:14

10:8
Num 25:1-9

10:9
Exod 17:2
Num 21:5-6

10:10
Num 14:2, 36;
16:41-49

10:13
1 Cor 1:9
2 Pet 2:9

9:26 Or *I am not just shadowboxing.*   **10:1** Greek *brothers.*   **10:3** Greek *spiritual;* also in 10:4.   **10:7** Exod 32:6.
10:9 Some manuscripts read *the Lord.*

• **9:24-27** Winning a race requires purpose and discipline. Paul uses this illustration to explain that the Christian life takes hard work, self-denial, and grueling preparation. As Christians, we are running toward our heavenly reward. The essential disciplines of prayer, Bible study, and worship equip us to run with vigor and stamina. Don't merely observe from the grandstand; don't just turn out to jog a couple of laps each morning. Train diligently—your spiritual progress depends upon it.

9:25 At times we must even give up something good in order to do what God wants. Each person's special duties determine the discipline and denial that he or she must accept. Without a goal, discipline is nothing but self-punishment. With the goal of pleasing God, our denial seems like nothing compared to the eternal, imperishable reward that will be ours.

• **9:27** When Paul says he might be disqualified, he does not mean that he could lose his salvation but rather that he could lose his privilege of telling others about Christ. It is easy to tell others how to live and then not to take our own advice. We must be careful to practice what we preach.

10:1ff In chapter 9 Paul used himself as an example of a mature Christian who disciplines himself to better serve God. In chapter 10, he uses Israel as an example of spiritual immaturity, shown in their overconfidence and lack of self-discipline.

• **10:1-5** The cloud and the sea mentioned here refer to Israel's escape from slavery in Egypt when God led them by a cloud and brought them safely through the Red Sea (Exodus 14). The miraculous food and water are the provisions God gave as they traveled through the wilderness (Exodus 15–16).

10:2 "They were all baptized in the cloud and the sea" means that just as we are united in Christ by baptism, so the Israelites were united under Moses' leadership and through the events of the Exodus.

• **10:7-10** The incident referred to in 10:7 is when the Israelites made a gold calf and worshiped it in the wilderness (Exodus 32). The incident in 10:8 is recorded in Numbers 25:1-9 when the Israelites worshiped Baal of Peor and engaged in sexual immorality with Moabite women. The reference in 10:9 is to the Israelites' complaint about their food (Numbers 21:5, 6). They put the Lord to the test by seeing how far they could go. In 10:10, Paul refers to when the people complained against Moses and Aaron, and the plague that resulted (Numbers 14:2, 36; 16:41-50). The angel of death is also referred to in Exodus 12:23.

• **10:11** Today's pressures make it easy to ignore or forget the lessons of the past. But Paul cautions us to remember the lessons the Israelites learned about God so we can avoid repeating their errors. The key to remembering is to study the Bible regularly so that these lessons remind us of how God wants us to live. We need not repeat their mistakes!

10:13 In a culture filled with moral depravity and sin-inducing pressures, Paul encouraged the Corinthians about temptation. He said that (1) temptations happen to everyone, so don't feel you've been singled out; (2) others have resisted temptation, and so can you; (3) any temptation can be resisted because God will show you a way out. God will help you in resisting temptation by helping you (1) recognize those people and situations that give you trouble, (2) run from anything you know is wrong, (3) choose to do only what is right, (4) pray for God's help, and (5) seek friends who love God and can offer help when you are tempted. Running from a tempting situation is your first step on the way to victory (see 2 Timothy 2:22).

10:14
1 Jn 5:21

10:16
Matt 26:26-28
Acts 2:42
1 Cor 11:23-26

10:17
Rom 12:5
1 Cor 12:27
Eph 4:16
Col 3:15

10:18
Lev 7:6, 14-15

10:20
Deut 32:17
Rev 9:20

10:21
2 Cor 6:15-16

10:22
Deut 32:16, 21

10:23
1 Cor 6:12

10:24
Rom 15:1-2

10:25
Acts 10:15
1 Cor 8:7

what others experience. And God is faithful. He will keep the temptation from becoming so strong that you can't stand up against it. When you are tempted, he will show you a way out so that you will not give in to it.

14 So, my dear friends, flee from the worship of idols. 15 You are reasonable people. Decide for yourselves if what I am about to say is true. 16 When we bless the cup at the Lord's Table, aren't we sharing in the benefits of the blood of Christ? And when we break the loaf of bread, aren't we sharing in the benefits of the body of Christ? 17 And we all eat from one loaf, showing that we are one body. 18 And think about the nation of Israel; all who eat the sacrifices are united by that act.

19 What am I trying to say? Am I saying that the idols to whom the pagans bring sacrifices are real gods and that these sacrifices are of some value? 20 No, not at all. What I am saying is that these sacrifices are offered to demons, not to God. And I don't want any of you to be partners with demons. 21 You cannot drink from the cup of the Lord and from the cup of demons, too. You cannot eat at the Lord's Table and at the table of demons, too. 22 What? Do you dare to rouse the Lord's jealousy as Israel did? Do you think we are stronger than he is?

23 You say, "I am allowed to do anything"—but not everything is helpful. You say, "I am allowed to do anything"—but not everything is beneficial. 24 Don't think only of your own good. Think of other Christians and what is best for them.

25 Here's what you should do. You may eat any meat that is sold in the marketplace.

MAKING CHOICES ON SENSITIVE ISSUES

If I choose one course of action:

. . . does it help my witness for Christ? (9:19–22)

. . . am I motivated by a desire to help others know Christ? (9:23; 10:33)

. . . does it help me do my best? (9:25)

. . . is it against a specific command in Scripture and would thus cause me to sin? (10:12)

. . . is it the best and most beneficial course of action? (10:23, 33)

. . . am I thinking only of myself, or do I truly care about the other person? (10:24)

. . . am I acting lovingly or selfishly? (10:28–31)

. . . does it glorify God? (10:31)

. . . will it cause someone else to sin? (10:32)

All of us make hundreds of choices every day. Most choices have no right or wrong attached to them—like what you wear or what you eat. But we always face decisions that carry a little more weight. We don't want to do wrong, and we don't want to cause others to do wrong, so how can we make such decisions?

10:14 Idol worship was the major expression of religion in Corinth. There were several pagan temples in the city, and they were very popular. The statues of wood or stone were not evil in themselves, but people gave them credit for what only God could do, such as provide good weather, crops, and children. Idolatry is still a serious problem today, but it takes a different form. We don't put our trust in statues of wood and stone but in paper money and plastic cards. Putting our trust in anything but God is idolatry. Our modern idols are those symbols of power, pleasure, or prestige that we so highly regard. When we understand contemporary parallels to idolatry, Paul's words to "flee from the worship of idols" become much more meaningful.

• **10:16-21** The idea of unity and fellowship with God through eating a sacrifice was strong in Judaism and Christianity as well as in paganism. In Old Testament days, when a Jew offered a sacrifice, he ate a part of that sacrifice as a way of restoring his unity with God, against whom he had sinned (Deuteronomy 12:17, 18). Similarly, Christians participate in Christ's once-for-all sacrifice at the Lord's Table when they eat the bread and drink from the cup, symbolizing his body and blood. Recent converts from paganism could not help being affected if they knowingly ate with pagans in their feasts the meat offered to idols.

• **10:21** As followers of Christ we must give him our total allegiance. We cannot, as Paul explains, have a part in "the cup of the Lord and . . . the cup of demons." Eating at the Lord's Table means communing with Christ and identifying with his death. Drinking from the cup of demons means identifying with Satan by worshiping or promoting pagan (or evil) activities. Are you leading two lives, trying to follow both Christ and the crowd? The Bible says that you can't do both at the same time.

• **10:23, 24** Sometimes it's hard to know when to defer to the weak believer. Paul gives a simple rule of thumb to help in making the decision: We should be sensitive and gracious. While some actions may not be wrong, they may not be in the best interest of others. While we have freedom in Christ, we shouldn't exercise our freedom at the cost of hurting a Christian brother or sister. We are not to consider only ourselves; we must be sensitive to others. For more on the proper attitude toward a weak believer, see the notes on 8:10-13 and Romans 14.

Don't ask whether or not it was offered to idols, and then your conscience won't be bothered. 26For "the earth is the Lord's, and everything in it."*

27If someone who isn't a Christian asks you home for dinner, go ahead; accept the invitation if you want to. Eat whatever is offered to you and don't ask any questions about it. Your conscience should not be bothered by this. 28But suppose someone warns you that this meat has been offered to an idol. Don't eat it, out of consideration for the conscience of the one who told you. 29It might not be a matter of conscience for you, but it is for the other person.

Now, why should my freedom be limited by what someone else thinks? 30If I can thank God for the food and enjoy it, why should I be condemned for eating it? 31Whatever you eat or drink or whatever you do, you must do all for the glory of God. 32Don't give offense to Jews or Gentiles or the church of God. 33That is the plan I follow, too. I try to please everyone in everything I do. I don't just do what I like or what is best for me, but what is best for them so they may be saved.

11 And you should follow my example, just as I follow Christ's.

3. Instruction on public worship

Proper Worship

2I am so glad, dear friends, that you always keep me in your thoughts and you are following the Christian teaching I passed on to you. 3But there is one thing I want you to know: A man is responsible to Christ, a woman is responsible to her husband, and

10:26 Ps 24:1.

10:27
Luke 10:8

10:28
Rom 14:16
1 Cor 8:7, 10-12

10:29
1 Cor 9:1, 19

10:30
1 Tim 4:4

10:31
Col 3:17

10:32
Matt 5:29
Acts 24:16
Rom 14:13
1 Cor 8:13

10:33
1 Cor 9:20-22

11:1
1 Cor 4:16

11:2
1 Cor 15:2-3
2 Thes 2:15; 3:6

11:3
Gen 3:16
1 Cor 3:23
Eph 5:23

10:25-27 Paul gave one answer to the dilemma: Buy whatever meat is sold at the market without asking whether or not it was offered to idols. It doesn't matter anyway, and no one's conscience would be bothered. When we become too worried about our every action, we become legalistic and cannot enjoy life. Everything belongs to God, and he has given us all things to enjoy. If we know something is a problem, then we can deal with it, but we don't need to go looking for problems.

• **10:28-33** Why should we be limited by another person's conscience? Simply because we are to do all things for God's glory, even our eating and drinking. Nothing we do should cause another believer to stumble. We do what is best for others, so that they might be saved. On the other hand, Christians should be careful not to have oversensitive consciences. Christian leaders and teachers should teach about the freedom we have in matters not expressly forbidden by Scripture.

• **10:31** Our actions must be motivated by God's love so that all we do will be for his glory. Keep this as a guiding principle by asking, Is this action glorifying God? or How can I honor God through this action?

10:33 Paul's criterion for all his actions was not what he liked best but what was best for those around him. The opposite approach would be (1) being insensitive and doing what we want, no matter who is hurt by it; (2) being oversensitive and doing nothing, for fear that someone may be displeased; (3) being a "yes person" by going along with everything, trying to gain approval from people rather than from God. In this age of "me first" and "looking out for number one," Paul's startling statement is a good standard. If we make the good of others one of our primary goals, we will develop a serving attitude that pleases God.

11:1 Why did Paul say, "Follow my example"? Paul wasn't being arrogant—he did not think of himself as sinless. At this time, however, the Corinthian believers did not know much about the life and ministry of Christ. Paul could not tell them to imitate Jesus because the Gospels had not yet been written, so they did not know what Jesus was like. The best way to point these new Christians to Christ was to point them to a Christian whom they trusted (see also Galatians 4:12; Philippians 3:17; 1 Thessalonians 1:6; 2:14; 2 Thessalonians 3:7, 9). Paul had been in Corinth

almost two years and had built a relationship of trust with many of these new believers.

11:2ff In this section Paul's main concern is irreverence in worship. We need to read it in the context of the situation in Corinth. The matter of wearing hats or head coverings, although seemingly insignificant, had become a big problem because two cultural backgrounds were colliding. Jewish women always covered their heads in worship. For a woman to uncover her head in public was a sign of loose morals. On the other hand, Greek women may have been used to worshiping without head coverings.

In this letter Paul had already spoken about divisions and disorder in the church. Both are involved in this issue. Paul's solution came from his desire for unity among church members and for appropriateness in the worship service. He accepted God's sovereignty in creating the rules for relationships.

• **11:2-16** This section focuses primarily on proper attitudes and conduct in worship, not on the marriage relationship or on the role of women in the church. While Paul's specific instructions may be cultural (women covering their heads in worship), the principles behind them are timeless: respect for spouse, reverence and appropriateness in worship, and focus of all of life on God. If you are doing something that might easily offend members and divide the church, then change your ways to promote church unity. Paul told the women who were not wearing head coverings to wear them, not because it was a scriptural command, but because it kept the congregation from dividing over a petty issue that served only to take people's minds off Christ.

• **11:3** The phrase "a woman is responsible to her husband" does not indicate the man's control or supremacy but rather his being her source. Because man was created first, the woman derives her existence from man, as man does from Christ and Christ from God. Evidently Paul was correcting some excesses in worship in which the emancipated Corinthian women were engaging.

11:3 The principle behind Paul's words is *submission*, which is a key element in the smooth functioning of any business, government, or family. God ordained submission in certain relationships to prevent chaos. It is essential to understand that submission is not surrender, withdrawal, or apathy. It does not mean inferiority, because God created all people in his image

11:5
Acts 21:9

11:7
Gen 1:26; 5:1; 9:6
Jas 3:9

11:8
Gen 2:21-23
1 Tim 2:13

11:9
Gen 2:18

11:12
Rom 11:36

11:16
1 Cor 7:17; 10:32

11:18
1 Cor 1:10-12; 3:3

11:19
1 Jn 2:19

11:21
2 Pet 2:13
Jude 1:12

11:22
1 Cor 10:32
Jas 2:6

11:23-25
†Matt 26:26-28
†Mark 14:22-24
†Luke 22:17-20

Christ is responsible to God. [4]A man dishonors Christ* if he covers his head while praying or prophesying. [5]But a woman dishonors her husband* if she prays or prophesies without a covering on her head, for this is the same as shaving her head. [6]Yes, if she refuses to wear a head covering, she should cut off all her hair. And since it is shameful for a woman to have her hair cut or her head shaved, then she should wear a covering.* [7]A man should not wear anything on his head when worshiping, for man is God's glory, made in God's own image, but woman is the glory of man. [8]For the first man didn't come from woman, but the first woman came from man. [9]And man was not made for woman's benefit, but woman was made for man. [10]So a woman should wear a covering on her head as a sign of authority because the angels are watching.

[11]But in relationships among the Lord's people, women are not independent of men, and men are not independent of women. [12]For although the first woman came from man, all men have been born from women ever since, and everything comes from God.

[13]What do you think about this? Is it right for a woman to pray to God in public without covering her head? [14]Isn't it obvious that it's disgraceful for a man to have long hair? [15]And isn't it obvious that long hair is a woman's pride and joy? For it has been given to her as a covering. [16]But if anyone wants to argue about this, all I can say is that we have no other custom than this, and all the churches of God feel the same way about it.

Order at the Lord's Supper

[17]But now when I mention this next issue, I cannot praise you. For it sounds as if more harm than good is done when you meet together. [18]First of all, I hear that there are divisions among you when you meet as a church, and to some extent I believe it. [19]But, of course, there must be divisions among you so that those of you who are right will be recognized!

[20]It's not the Lord's Supper you are concerned about when you come together. [21]For I am told that some of you hurry to eat your own meal without sharing with others. As a result, some go hungry while others get drunk. [22]What? Is this really true? Don't you have your own homes for eating and drinking? Or do you really want to disgrace the church of God and shame the poor? What am I supposed to say about these things? Do you want me to praise you? Well, I certainly do not!

[23]For this is what the Lord himself said, and I pass it on to you just as I received it. On the night when he was betrayed, the Lord Jesus took a loaf of bread, [24]and when he had

11:4 Greek *his head.*   **11:5** Greek *her head.*   **11:6** Or *then she should have long hair.*

---

and all have equal value. Submission is mutual commitment and cooperation.

Thus, God calls for submission among *equals*. He did not make the man superior; he made a way for a husband and wife to work together. Jesus Christ, although equal with God the Father, submitted to him to carry out the plan for salvation. Likewise, although equal to man under God, the wife should submit to her husband for the sake of their marriage and family. Submission between equals is submission by choice, not by force. We serve God in these relationships by willingly submitting to others in our church, to our spouses, and to our government leaders.

● **11:9-11** God created lines of authority in order for his created world to function smoothly. Although there must be lines of authority even in marriage, there should *not* be lines of superiority. God created men and women with unique and complementary characteristics. One sex is not better than the other. We must not let the issue of authority and submission become a wedge to destroy oneness in marriage. Instead, we should use our unique gifts to strengthen our marriages and to glorify God.

11:10 This verse may mean that the woman should wear a covering on her head as a sign that she is under the man's authority. This is a fact even the angels understand as they observe Christians in worship. See the note on 11:2ff for an explanation of head coverings.

● **11:14, 15** In talking about head coverings and length of hair, Paul is saying that believers should look and behave in ways that are honorable in their own culture. In many cultures long hair on men is considered appropriate and masculine. In Corinth, it was

thought to be a sign of male prostitution in the pagan temples. And women with short hair were labeled prostitutes. Paul was saying that in the Corinthian culture, Christian women should keep their hair long. If short hair on women was a sign of prostitution, then a Christian woman with short hair would find it difficult to be a believable witness for Jesus Christ. Paul wasn't saying we should adopt all the practices of our culture but that we should avoid appearances and behavior that detract from our ultimate goal of being witnesses for Jesus Christ.

11:17-34 The Lord's Supper (11:20) is a visible representation symbolizing the death of Christ for our sins. It reminds us of Christ's death and the glorious hope of his return. Our participation in it strengthens our faith through fellowship with Christ and with other believers.

11:18, 19 Paul acknowledges that there are differences among church members. When they develop into self-willed divisions, however, they are destructive to the congregation. Those who cause division only serve to highlight those who are genuine believers.

● **11:21, 22** When the Lord's Supper was celebrated in the early church, it included a feast or fellowship meal followed by the celebration of Communion. In the church in Corinth, the fellowship meal had become a time when some ate and drank excessively while others went hungry. There was little sharing and caring. This certainly did not demonstrate the unity and love that should characterize the church, nor was it a preparation for Communion. Paul condemned these actions and reminded the church of the real purpose of the Lord's Supper.

given thanks, he broke it and said, " This is my body, which is given* for you. Do this in remembrance of me." [25]In the same way, he took the cup of wine after supper, saying, " This cup is the new covenant between God and you, sealed by the shedding of my blood. Do this in remembrance of me as often as you drink it." [26]For every time you eat this bread and drink this cup, you are announcing the Lord's death until he comes again.

[27]So if anyone eats this bread or drinks this cup of the Lord unworthily, that person is guilty of sinning against the body and the blood of the Lord. [28]That is why you should examine yourself before eating the bread and drinking from the cup. [29]For if you eat the bread or drink the cup unworthily, not honoring the body of Christ,* you are eating and drinking God's judgment upon yourself. [30]That is why many of you are weak and sick and some have even died.

[31]But if we examine ourselves, we will not be examined by God and judged in this way. [32]But when we are judged and disciplined by the Lord, we will not be condemned with the world. [33]So, dear brothers and sisters,* when you gather for the Lord's Supper, wait for each other. [34]If you are really hungry, eat at home so you won't bring judgment upon yourselves when you meet together.

I'll give you instructions about the other matters after I arrive.

Spiritual Gifts

12 And now, dear brothers and sisters,* I will write about the special abilities the Holy Spirit gives to each of us, for I must correct your misunderstandings about them. [2]You know that when you were still pagans you were led astray and swept along

11:25
Luke 22:20
1 Cor 10:16
2 Cor 3:6

11:26
Matt 26:69

11:27
Heb 10:29

11:28
Matt 26:22
2 Cor 13:5

11:31
1 Jn 1:9

11:32
Ps 94:12
Heb 12:5-6

11:34
1 Cor 4:19

12:1
1 Cor 14:1

12:2
Hab 2:18-19
1 Thes 1:9

11:24 Some manuscripts read *broken.*   **11:29** Greek *the body;* some manuscripts read *the Lord's body.*   **11:33** Greek *brothers.*   **12:1** Greek *brothers.*

11:24, 25 What does the Lord's Supper mean? The early church remembered that Jesus instituted the Lord's Supper on the night of the Passover meal (Luke 22:13-20). Just as Passover celebrated deliverance from slavery in Egypt, so the Lord's Supper celebrates deliverance from sin by Christ's death.

Christians pose several different possibilities for what Christ meant when he said, "This is my body." (1) Some believe that the bread and wine actually become Christ's physical blood and body. (2) Others believe that the bread and wine remain unchanged, but Christ is spiritually present with the bread and wine. (3) Still others believe that the bread and wine symbolize Christ's body and blood. Christians generally agree, however, that participating in the Lord's Supper is an important element in the Christian faith and that Christ's presence, however we understand it, strengthens us spiritually.

11:25 What is this new covenant? In the old covenant, people could approach God only through the priests and the sacrificial system. Jesus' death on the cross ushered in the new covenant or agreement between God and us. Now all people can personally approach God and communicate with him. The people of Israel first entered into this agreement after their exodus from Egypt (Exodus 24), and it was designed to point to the day when Jesus Christ would come. The new covenant completes, rather than replaces, the old covenant, fulfilling everything the old covenant looked forward to (see Jeremiah 31:31-34). Eating the bread and drinking the cup shows that we are remembering Christ's death for us and renewing our commitment to serve him.

11:25 Jesus said, "Do this in remembrance of me as often as you drink it." How do we remember Christ in the Lord's Supper? By thinking about what he did and why he did it. If the Lord's Supper becomes just a ritual or a pious habit, it no longer celebrates Christ's death, and it loses its significance.

● **11:27ff** Paul gives specific instructions on how the Lord's Supper should be observed. (1) We should take the Lord's Supper thoughtfully because we are proclaiming that Christ died for our sins (11:26). (2) We should take it worthily, with due reverence and respect (11:27). (3) We should examine ourselves for any unconfessed sin or resentful attitude and be properly prepared (11:28). (4) We should be considerate of others, waiting until

everyone is there and then eating in an orderly and unified manner (11:33).

● **11:27-34** When Paul said that no one should take the Lord's Supper unworthily, he was speaking to the church members who were participating in it without thinking of its meaning. Those who did so were "guilty of sinning against the body and the blood of the Lord." Instead of honoring his sacrifice, they were sharing in the guilt of those who crucified Christ. In reality, *no one* is worthy to take the Lord's Supper. We are all sinners saved by grace. This is why we should prepare ourselves for Communion through healthy introspection, confession of sin, and resolution of differences with others. These actions remove the barriers that affect our relationship with Christ and with other believers. Awareness of your sin should not keep you away from Communion but drive you to participate in it.

11:29 To not honor the "body of Christ" means not understanding what the Lord's Supper means and not distinguishing it from a normal meal. Those who do so condemn themselves (see 11:27).

11:30 That some of the people had died may have been a special supernatural judgment on the Corinthian church. This type of disciplinary judgment highlights the seriousness of the Communion service. The Lord's Supper is not to be taken lightly; this new covenant cost Jesus his life. It is not a meaningless ritual, but a sacrament given by Christ to help strengthen our faith.

11:34 People should come to this meal desiring to fellowship with other believers and prepare for the Lord's Supper to follow, not to fill up on a big dinner. "If you are really hungry, eat at home" means that they should eat dinner beforehand so as to come to the fellowship meal in the right frame of mind.

12:1ff The spiritual gifts given to each person by the Holy Spirit are special abilities that are to be used to minister to the needs of the body of believers. This chapter is not an exhaustive list of spiritual gifts (see Romans 12; Ephesians 4; 1 Peter 4:10, 11 for more examples). There are many gifts; people have different gifts; some people have more than one gift, and one gift is not superior to another. All spiritual gifts come from the Holy Spirit, and their purpose is to build up Christ's body, the church.

12:1ff Instead of building up and unifying the Corinthian church, the issue of spiritual gifts was splitting it. Spiritual gifts

12:3
John 13:13
1 Jn 4:2-3

12:4
Rom 12:6
Eph 4:4
Heb 2:4

12:6
Eph 4:6

12:8
1 Cor 2:6

12:9
Matt 17:19-20

12:10
Acts 2:4
Rom 12:6
1 Cor 14:26-32
Gal 3:5
Eph 4:5
1 Jn 4:1

12:11
Rom 12:6-8
Eph 4:7

12:12
Rom 12:4-5
1 Cor 10:17; 12:27

12:13
John 7:37-39
Gal 3:28
Eph 2:18
Col 3:11

12:18
1 Cor 12:28

in worshiping speechless idols. ³So I want you to know how to discern what is truly from God: No one speaking by the Spirit of God can curse Jesus, and no one is able to say, "Jesus is Lord," except by the Holy Spirit.

⁴Now there are different kinds of spiritual gifts, but it is the same Holy Spirit who is the source of them all. ⁵There are different kinds of service in the church, but it is the same Lord we are serving. ⁶There are different ways God works in our lives, but it is the same God who does the work through all of us. ⁷A spiritual gift is given to each of us as a means of helping the entire church.

⁸To one person the Spirit gives the ability to give wise advice; to another he gives the gift of special knowledge. ⁹The Spirit gives special faith to another, and to someone else he gives the power to heal the sick. ¹⁰He gives one person the power to perform miracles, and to another the ability to prophesy. He gives someone else the ability to know whether it is really the Spirit of God or another spirit that is speaking. Still another person is given the ability to speak in unknown languages,* and another is given the ability to interpret what is being said. ¹¹It is the one and only Holy Spirit who distributes these gifts. He alone decides which gift each person should have.

One Body with Many Parts

¹²The human body has many parts, but the many parts make up only one body. So it is with the body of Christ. ¹³Some of us are Jews, some are Gentiles, some are slaves, and some are free. But we have all been baptized into Christ's body by one Spirit, and we have all received the same Spirit.*

¹⁴Yes, the body has many different parts, not just one part. ¹⁵If the foot says, "I am not a part of the body because I am not a hand," that does not make it any less a part of the body. ¹⁶And if the ear says, "I am not part of the body because I am only an ear and not an eye," would that make it any less a part of the body? ¹⁷Suppose the whole body were an eye—then how would you hear? Or if your whole body were just one big ear, how could you smell anything?

¹⁸But God made our bodies with many parts, and he has put each part just where he wants it. ¹⁹What a strange thing a body would be if it had only one part! ²⁰Yes, there are

12:10 Or *in tongues;* also in 12:28, 30.   **12:13** Greek *we were all given one Spirit to drink.*

---

had become symbols of spiritual power, causing rivalries. Some people thought they were more "spiritual" than others because of their gifts. This was a terrible misuse of spiritual gifts because their purpose is always to help the church function more effectively, not to divide it. We can be divisive if we insist on using our gifts our own way without being sensitive to others. We must never use our gifts as a means of manipulating others or serving our own self-interests.

12:3 Anyone can claim to speak for God, and the world is full of false teachers. Paul gives us a test to help us discern whether or not a messenger is really from God: Does he or she confess Christ as Lord? Don't naively accept the words of all who claim to speak for God; test their credentials by finding out what they teach about Christ.

12:9 All Christians have faith. Some, however, have the spiritual gift of faith, which is an unusual measure of trust in the power of God.

12:10, 11 Prophecy is not just a prediction about the future; it can also mean preaching God's Word with power. Paul discusses speaking in unknown languages and interpreting them in more detail in chapter 14. No matter what gifts a person has, each gift is given by the Holy Spirit. We are responsible to use and sharpen our gifts, but we can take no credit for what God has freely given us.

• **12:12** Paul compares the body of Christ to a human body. Each part has a specific function that is necessary to the body as a whole. The parts are different for a purpose, and in their differences they must work together. Christians must avoid two common errors: (1) being proud of their abilities, or (2) thinking they have nothing to give to the body of believers. Instead of

comparing ourselves to one another, we should use our different gifts, together, to spread the Good News of salvation.

• **12:13** The church is composed of many types of people from a variety of backgrounds with a multitude of gifts and abilities. It is easy for these differences to divide people, as was the case in Corinth. But despite the differences, all believers have one thing in common—faith in Christ. On this essential truth the church finds unity. All believers are baptized by one Holy Spirit into one body of believers, the church. We don't lose our individual identities, but we have an overriding oneness in Christ. When we become a Christian, the Holy Spirit takes up residence in us, and we are born into God's family. "We have all received the same Spirit" means that each of us has received the same Holy Spirit. As members of God's family, we may have different interests and gifts, but we are united by the Spirit into one spiritual body.

• **12:14-24** Using the analogy of the body, Paul emphasizes the importance of each church member (see the note on 12:12). If a seemingly insignificant part is taken away, the whole body becomes less effective. Thinking that your gift is more important than someone else's is an expression of spiritual pride. We should not look down on those who seem unimportant, and we should not be jealous of others who have more visible gifts. Instead, we should use the gifts we have been given and encourage others to use theirs. If we don't, the body of believers will be less effective.

many parts, but only one body. [21] The eye can never say to the hand, "I don't need you." The head can't say to the feet, "I don't need you."

[22] In fact, some of the parts that seem weakest and least important are really the most necessary. [23] And the parts we regard as less honorable are those we clothe with the greatest care. So we carefully protect from the eyes of others those parts that should not be seen, [24] while other parts do not require this special care. So God has put the body together in such a way that extra honor and care are given to those parts that have less dignity. [25] This makes for harmony among the members, so that all the members care for each other equally. [26] If one part suffers, all the parts suffer with it, and if one part is honored, all the parts are glad.

[27] Now all of you together are Christ's body, and each one of you is a separate and necessary part of it. [28] Here is a list of some of the members that God has placed in the body of Christ:

first are apostles,
second are prophets,
third are teachers,
then those who do miracles,
those who have the gift of healing,
those who can help others,
those who can get others to work together,
those who speak in unknown languages.

[29] Is everyone an apostle? Of course not. Is everyone a prophet? No. Are all teachers? Does everyone have the power to do miracles? [30] Does everyone have the gift of healing? Of course not. Does God give all of us the ability to speak in unknown languages? Can everyone interpret unknown languages? No! [31] And in any event, you should desire the most helpful gifts.

Love Is the Greatest
First, however, let me tell you about something else that is better than any of them!

13 If I could speak in any language in heaven or on earth* but didn't love others, I would only be making meaningless noise like a loud gong or a clanging cymbal. [2] If I had the gift of prophecy, and if I knew all the mysteries of the future and knew everything about everything, but didn't love others, what good would I be? And if I had the gift of faith so that I could speak to a mountain and make it move, without love I would be no good to anybody. [3] If I gave everything I have to the poor and even sacrificed my body, I could boast about it;* but if I didn't love others, I would be of no value whatsoever.

[4] Love is patient and kind. Love is not jealous or boastful or proud [5] or rude. Love does not demand its own way. Love is not irritable, and it keeps no record of when it has been wronged. [6] It is never glad about injustice but rejoices whenever the truth wins

13:1 Greek *in tongues of people and angels.* 13:3 Some manuscripts read *and even gave my body to be burned.*

12:27
Rom 12:5
Eph 1:23; 4:12
Col 1:18, 24

12:28
Rom 12:6-8
Eph 4:11-12

12:31
1 Cor 14:1, 39

13:1
1 Tim 1:5

13:2
Matt 17:20; 21:21
Mark 11:23
1 Cor 12:9

13:3
Matt 6:2

13:4
1 Pet 4:8

13:5
1 Cor 10:24
Phil 2:4

13:6
2 Thes 2:12
2 Jn 1:4
3 Jn 1:3-4

● **12:25, 26** What is your response when a fellow Christian is honored? How do you respond when someone is suffering? We are to be happy with those who are happy, and if they are sad, share their sorrow (Romans 12:15). Too often, unfortunately, we are jealous of those who rejoice and apathetic toward those who weep. Believers are in the world together—there is no such thing as private or individualistic Christianity. We need to get involved in the lives of others and not just enjoy our own relationship with God.

12:30 Paul discusses the subject of speaking in and interpreting unknown languages in more detail in chapter 14.

12:31 The most helpful gifts are those that are beneficial to the body of Christ. Paul has already made it clear that one gift is not superior to another, but he urges the believers to discover how they can serve Christ's body with the gifts God has given them. Your spiritual gifts are not for your own self-advancement. They were given to you for serving God and enhancing the spiritual growth of the body of believers.

● **13:1ff** In chapter 12 Paul gave evidence of the Corinthians' lack of love in the utilization of spiritual gifts; chapter 13 defines real love; and chapter 14 shows how love works. Love is more important than all the spiritual gifts exercised in the church body. Great faith, acts of dedication or sacrifice, and miracle-working power have little effect without love. Love makes our actions and gifts useful. Although people have different gifts, love is available to everyone.

● **13:4-7** Our society confuses love and lust. Unlike lust, God's kind of love is directed outward toward others, not inward toward ourselves. It is utterly unselfish. This kind of love goes against our natural inclinations. It is impossible to have this love unless God helps us set aside our own natural desires so that we can love and not expect anything in return. Thus, the more we become like Christ, the more love we will show to others.

13:7
Prov 10:12
Rom 15:1
1 Pet 4:8

13:10
Phil 3:12

13:11
Ps 131:2

13:12
2 Cor 5:7
1 Jn 3:2

13:13
Matt 22:37-40
Gal 5:5-6
1 Thes 1:3
1 Jn 4:16

14:1
Matt 22:37-40
Rom 12:6
1 Cor 12:1, 31;
14:39; 16:14
Eph 5:2
Col 3:14
1 Tim 1:5
Jas 2:8

14:2
Mark 16:17
Acts 2:4; 10:46-47;
19:6

14:3
Rom 14:19

14:4
1 Cor 14:18-19,
26-28

14:5
Num 11:29

14:6
Rom 6:17
Eph 1:17

14:8
Num 10:9
Jer 4:19

out. ⁷Love never gives up, never loses faith, is always hopeful, and endures through every circumstance.

⁸Love will last forever, but prophecy and speaking in unknown languages* and special knowledge will all disappear. ⁹Now we know only a little, and even the gift of prophecy reveals little! ¹⁰But when the end comes, these special gifts will all disappear.

¹¹It's like this: When I was a child, I spoke and thought and reasoned as a child does. But when I grew up, I put away childish things. ¹²Now we see things imperfectly as in a poor mirror, but then we will see everything with perfect clarity.* All that I know now is partial and incomplete, but then I will know everything completely, just as God knows me now.

¹³There are three things that will endure—faith, hope, and love—and the greatest of these is love.

The Gifts of Tongues and Prophecy

14 Let love be your highest goal, but also desire the special abilities the Spirit gives, especially the gift of prophecy. ²For if your gift is the ability to speak in tongues,* you will be talking to God but not to people, since they won't be able to understand you. You will be speaking by the power of the Spirit, but it will all be mysterious. ³But one who prophesies is helping others grow in the Lord, encouraging and comforting them. ⁴A person who speaks in tongues is strengthened personally in the Lord, but one who speaks a word of prophecy strengthens the entire church.

⁵I wish you all had the gift of speaking in tongues, but even more I wish you were all able to prophesy. For prophecy is a greater and more useful gift than speaking in tongues, unless someone interprets what you are saying so that the whole church can get some good out of it.

⁶Dear brothers and sisters,* if I should come to you talking in an unknown language,* how would that help you? But if I bring you some revelation or some special knowledge or some prophecy or some teaching—that is what will help you. ⁷Even musical instruments like the flute or the harp, though they are lifeless, are examples of the need for speaking in plain language. For no one will recognize the melody unless the notes are played clearly. ⁸And if the bugler doesn't sound a clear call, how will the soldiers know they are being called to battle? ⁹And it's the same for you. If you talk to people in a language they don't understand, how will they know what you mean? You might as well be talking to an empty room.

¹⁰There are so many different languages in the world, and all are excellent for those

13:8 Or *in tongues.*   **13:12** Greek *see face to face.*   **14:2** Or *in unknown languages;* also in 14:4, 5, 13, 14, 18, 22, 28, 39.   **14:6a** Greek *brothers;* also in 14:20, 26, 39.   **14:6b** Or *in tongues;* also in 14:19, 23, 26, 27.

13:10   God gives us spiritual gifts in order to build up, serve, and strengthen fellow Christians—the church. In eternity, we will be made perfect and complete and will be in the very presence of God. We will no longer need spiritual gifts, so they will come to an end.

• **13:12**   Paul offers a glimpse into the future to give us hope that one day we will be complete when we see God face to face. This truth should strengthen our faith. We don't have all the answers now, but one day we will. Someday we will see Christ in person and be able to see with God's perspective.

• **13:13**   In morally corrupt Corinth, love had become a mixed-up term with little meaning. Today people are still confused about love. Love is the greatest of all human qualities, and it is an attribute of God himself (1 John 4:8). Love involves unselfish service to others; to show it gives evidence that you care. *Faith* is the foundation and content of God's message; *hope* is the attitude and focus; *love* is the action. When faith and hope are in line, you are free to love completely because you understand how God loves.

• **14:1**   Prophecy may involve predicting future events, but its main purpose is to communicate God's message to people, providing insight, warning, correction, and encouragement.

• **14:2**   The gift of speaking in tongues (unknown languages) was a concern of the Corinthian church because the use of the gift

had caused disorder in worship. Speaking in tongues is a legitimate gift of the Holy Spirit, but the Corinthian believers were using it as a sign of spiritual superiority rather than as a means to spiritual unity. Spiritual gifts are beneficial only when they are properly used to help everyone in the church. We should not exercise them only to make *ourselves* feel good.

14:2ff   Paul makes several points about speaking in tongues: (1) It is a spiritual gift from God (14:2); (2) it is a desirable gift even though it isn't a requirement of faith (12:28-31); (3) it is less important than prophecy and teaching (14:4). Although Paul himself spoke in tongues, he stresses prophecy (preaching) because it benefits the whole church, while speaking in tongues primarily benefits the speaker. Public worship must be understandable and edifying to the whole church.

14:7-12   As musical instruments must clearly play each note in order for the music to be recognized, so Paul says words must be preached in the hearers' language in order to be helpful. Because there are many languages in the world (14:10), people sometimes can't understand each other. It is the same with speaking in tongues. Although this gift is helpful to many people in private worship as well as in public worship (with interpretation), Paul says that he would rather speak 5 words that his hearers can understand than 10,000 that they cannot (14:19).

who understand them, [11] but to me they mean nothing. I will not understand people who speak those languages, and they will not understand me. [12] Since you are so eager to have spiritual gifts, ask God for those that will be of real help to the whole church.

14:12
Rom 14:19
1 Cor 12:1

[13] So anyone who has the gift of speaking in tongues should pray also for the gift of interpretation in order to tell people plainly what has been said. [14] For if I pray in tongues, my spirit is praying, but I don't understand what I am saying.

14:13
1 Cor 12:10

[15] Well then, what shall I do? I will do both. I will pray in the spirit,* and I will pray in words I understand. I will sing in the spirit, and I will sing in words I understand. [16] For if you praise God only in the spirit, how can those who don't understand you praise God along with you? How can they join you in giving thanks when they don't understand what you are saying? [17] You will be giving thanks very nicely, no doubt, but it doesn't help the other people present.

14:15
Eph 5:19
Col 3:16

14:16
1 Chr 16:36
Neh 8:6
Ps 106:48
Rev 5:14; 7:12

[18] I thank God that I speak in tongues more than all of you. [19] But in a church meeting I would much rather speak five understandable words that will help others than ten thousand words in an unknown language.

14:17
Rom 14:19

[20] Dear brothers and sisters, don't be childish in your understanding of these things. Be innocent as babies when it comes to evil, but be mature and wise in understanding matters of this kind. [21] It is written in the Scriptures,*

14:20
Eph 4:14
Heb 5:12

14:21
Deut 28:49
†Isa 28:11-12
John 10:34

> "I will speak to my own people
> through unknown languages
> and through the lips of foreigners.
> But even then, they will not listen to me,"*
> says the Lord.

[22] So you see that speaking in tongues is a sign, not for believers, but for unbelievers; prophecy, however, is for the benefit of believers, not unbelievers. [23] Even so, if unbelievers or people who don't understand these things come into your meeting and hear everyone talking in an unknown language, they will think you are crazy. [24] But if all of you are prophesying, and unbelievers or people who don't understand these things come into your meeting, they will be convicted of sin, and they will be condemned by what you say. [25] As they listen, their secret thoughts will be laid bare, and they will fall down on their knees and worship God, declaring, "God is really here among you."

14:22
1 Cor 14:1

14:23
Acts 2:13

14:24
John 16:8

14:25
Isa 45:14
Zech 8:23

A Call to Orderly Worship

[26] Well, my brothers and sisters, let's summarize what I am saying. When you meet, one will sing, another will teach, another will tell some special revelation God has given, one will speak in an unknown language, while another will interpret what is said. But everything that is done must be useful to all and build them up in the Lord. [27] No more than two or three should speak in an unknown language. They must speak one at a time, and someone must be ready to interpret what they are saying. [28] But if no one is present who can interpret, they must be silent in your church meeting and speak in tongues to God privately.

14:26
Rom 14:19
1 Cor 12:7-10
Eph 4:12; 5:19

14:27
1 Cor 14:2, 5, 13

[29] Let two or three prophesy, and let the others evaluate what is said. [30] But if someone is prophesying and another person receives a revelation from the Lord, the one who is

14:29
1 Cor 12:10
1 Thes 5:19-21

14:15 Or *in the Spirit;* also in 14:15b, 16.   **14:21a** Greek *in the law.*   **14:21b** Isa 28:11-12.

14:13-20 If a person has the gift of speaking in tongues, he should also pray for the gift of knowing what he has said (interpretation) so he can tell people afterward. This way, the entire church will be edified by this gift.

14:15 There is a proper place for the intellect in Christianity. In praying and singing, both the mind and the spirit are to be fully engaged. When we sing, we should also think about the meaning of the words. When we pour out our feelings to God in prayer, we should not turn off our capacity to think. True Christianity is neither barren intellectualism nor thoughtless emotionalism. See also Ephesians 1:17, 18; Philippians 1:9-11; Colossians 1:9.

• **14:22-25** The way the Corinthians were speaking in tongues was helping no one because believers did not understand what was being said, and unbelievers thought that the people speaking in tongues were crazy. Speaking in tongues was supposed to be a *sign* to unbelievers (as it was in Acts 2). After speaking in tongues, believers were supposed to explain what was said and give the credit to God. The unsaved people would then be convinced of a spiritual reality and motivated to look further into the Christian faith. While this is one way to reach unbelievers, Paul says that clear preaching is usually better (14:5).

• **14:26ff** Everything done in worship services must be beneficial to the worshipers. This principle touches every aspect—singing, preaching, and the exercise of spiritual gifts. Those contributing to the service (singers, speakers, readers) must have love as their chief motivation, speaking useful words or participating in a way that will strengthen the faith of other believers.

14:32
1 Jn 4:1

14:33
1 Cor 7:17

14:34
Gen 3:16
Eph 5:22
Col 3:18
1 Tim 2:11-12
Titus 2:5

14:37
2 Cor 10:7
1 Jn 4:6

14:39
1 Cor 12:31
1 Thes 5:20

14:40
1 Cor 14:33
Col 2:5

15:3
Isa 53:5-9
Luke 24:25-27
1 Pet 2:24

15:4
Ps 16:10
Hos 6:2
Jon 1:17
Luke 24:25-27
John 2:21-22
Acts 2:24-32

15:5
Matt 28:16-17
Mark 16:14
Luke 24:34, 36-43
John 20:19

15:8
Acts 9:3-6
Gal 1:16

speaking must stop. ³¹In this way, all who prophesy will have a turn to speak, one after the other, so that everyone will learn and be encouraged. ³²Remember that people who prophesy are in control of their spirit and can wait their turn. ³³For God is not a God of disorder but of peace, as in all the other churches.*

³⁴Women should be silent during the church meetings. It is not proper for them to speak. They should be submissive, just as the law says. ³⁵If they have any questions to ask, let them ask their husbands at home, for it is improper for women to speak in church meetings.*

³⁶Do you think that the knowledge of God's word begins and ends with you Corinthians? Well, you are mistaken! ³⁷If you claim to be a prophet or think you are very spiritual, you should recognize that what I am saying is a command from the Lord himself. ³⁸But if you do not recognize this, you will not be recognized.*

³⁹So, dear brothers and sisters, be eager to prophesy, and don't forbid speaking in tongues. ⁴⁰But be sure that everything is done properly and in order.

4. Instruction on the resurrection

The Resurrection of Christ

15 Now let me remind you, dear brothers and sisters,* of the Good News I preached to you before. You welcomed it then and still do now, for your faith is built on this wonderful message. ²And it is this Good News that saves you if you firmly believe it—unless, of course, you believed something that was never true in the first place.

³I passed on to you what was most important and what had also been passed on to me—that Christ died for our sins, just as the Scriptures said. ⁴He was buried, and he was raised from the dead on the third day, as the Scriptures said. ⁵He was seen by Peter* and then by the twelve apostles. ⁶After that, he was seen by more than five hundred of his followers* at one time, most of whom are still alive, though some have died by now. ⁷Then he was seen by James and later by all the apostles. ⁸Last of all, I saw him, too, long after the others, as though I had been born at the wrong time. ⁹For I am the least of

14:33 The phrase *as in all the other churches* could be joined to the beginning of 14:34.   **14:35** Some manuscripts place verses 34-35 after 14:40.   **14:38** Some manuscripts read *If you are ignorant of this, stay in your ignorance.*
15:1 Greek *brothers;* also in 15:31, 50, 58.   **15:5** Greek *Cephas.*   **15:6** Greek *the brothers.*

• **14:33** In worship, everything must be done with propriety and in an orderly fashion, especially when the gifts of the Holy Spirit are being exercised. When there is chaos and disorder in the church, God cannot work, for he is not a God of confusion but of peace.

14:34, 35 Does this mean that women should not speak in church services today? It is clear from 11:5 that women prayed and prophesied in public worship. It is also clear in chapters 12–14 that women are given spiritual gifts and are encouraged to exercise them in the body of Christ. Women have much to contribute and can participate in worship services.

In the Corinthian culture, women were not allowed to confront men in public. Apparently some of the women who had become Christians thought that their Christian freedom gave them the right to question the men in public worship. This was causing division in the church. In addition, women of that day did not receive formal religious education as did the men. Women may have been raising questions in the worship services that could have been answered at home without disrupting the services. Paul was asking the women not to flaunt their Christian freedom during worship. The purpose of Paul's words was to promote unity, not to teach about women's roles in the church.

14:40 Worship is vital to the life of an individual and to the whole church. Our church services should be conducted in an orderly way so that we can worship, be taught, and be prepared to serve God. Those who are responsible for planning worship should make sure it has order and direction rather than chaos and confusion.

15:2 Most churches contain people who do not yet believe. Some are moving in the direction of belief, and others are simply pretending. Imposters, however, are not to be removed (see Matthew 13:28, 29), for that is the Lord's work alone. The Good News about Jesus Christ will save us *if* we firmly believe it and faithfully follow it.

• **15:5-8** There will always be people who say that Jesus didn't rise from the dead. Paul assures us that many people saw Jesus after his resurrection: Peter; the disciples (the Twelve); more than 500 Christian believers (most of whom were still alive when Paul wrote this, although some had died); James (Jesus' half brother); all the apostles; and finally Paul himself. The Resurrection is a historical fact. Don't be discouraged by doubters who deny the Resurrection. Be filled with hope because of the knowledge that one day you, and they, will see the living proof when Christ returns. (For more evidence on the Resurrection, see the chart in Mark 16.)

15:7 This James is Jesus' half brother, who at first did not believe that Jesus was the Messiah (John 7:5). After seeing the resurrected Christ, he became a believer and ultimately a leader of the church in Jerusalem (Acts 15:13). James wrote the New Testament book of James.

15:8, 9 Paul's most important credential of his apostleship was that he was an eyewitness of the risen Christ (see Acts 9:3-6). The other apostles saw Christ in the flesh. Paul was in the next generation of believers—yet Christ appeared to him.

15:9, 10 As a zealous Pharisee, Paul had been an enemy of the Christian church—even to the point of capturing and persecuting believers (see Acts 9:1-3). Thus, he felt unworthy to be called an apostle of Christ. Though undoubtedly the most influential of the apostles, Paul was deeply humble. He knew that he had worked hard and accomplished much but only because God had poured kindness and grace upon him. True humility is not convincing yourself that you are worthless but recognizing God's work in you. It is having God's perspective on who you are and acknowledging his grace in developing your abilities.

all the apostles, and I am not worthy to be called an apostle after the way I persecuted the church of God. ¹⁰But whatever I am now, it is all because God poured out his special favor on me—and not without results. For I have worked harder than all the other apostles, yet it was not I but God who was working through me by his grace. ¹¹So it makes no difference whether I preach or they preach. The important thing is that you believed what we preached to you.

The Resurrection of the Dead

¹²But tell me this—since we preach that Christ rose from the dead, why are some of you saying there will be no resurrection of the dead? ¹³For if there is no resurrection of the dead, then Christ has not been raised either. ¹⁴And if Christ was not raised, then all our preaching is useless, and your trust in God is useless. ¹⁵And we apostles would all be lying about God, for we have said that God raised Christ from the grave, but that can't be true if there is no resurrection of the dead. ¹⁶If there is no resurrection of the dead, then Christ has not been raised. ¹⁷And if Christ has not been raised, then your faith is useless, and you are still under condemnation for your sins. ¹⁸In that case, all who have died believing in Christ have perished! ¹⁹And if we have hope in Christ only for this life, we are the most miserable people in the world.

²⁰But the fact is that Christ has been raised from the dead. He has become the first of a great harvest of those who will be raised to life again.

²¹So you see, just as death came into the world through a man, Adam, now the resurrection from the dead has begun through another man, Christ. ²²Everyone dies because all of us are related to Adam, the first man. But all who are related to Christ, the other man, will be given new life. ²³But there is an order to this resurrection: Christ was raised first; then when Christ comes back, all his people will be raised.

²⁴After that the end will come, when he will turn the Kingdom over to God the Father, having put down all enemies of every kind.* ²⁵For Christ must reign until he humbles all his enemies beneath his feet. ²⁶And the last enemy to be destroyed is death. ²⁷For the Scriptures say, "God has given him authority over all things."* (Of course, when it says "authority over all things," it does not include God himself, who gave Christ his authority.) ²⁸Then, when he has conquered all things, the Son will present himself to

15:9
Acts 8:3
2 Cor 12:11
Eph 3:8

15:10
2 Cor 6:1; 11:5, 23

15:12
Acts 17:32; 23:8
2 Tim 2:18

15:17
Rom 4:25

15:20
Col 1:18
1 Pet 1:3
Rev 1:5

15:21
Rom 5:12, 18

15:22
Rom 5:14-18

15:23
1 Thes 4:16

15:24
Dan 2:44; 7:14

15:25
Ps 110:1
Isa 9:7
Matt 22:44

15:26
2 Tim 1:10
Rev 20:14; 21:4

15:27
†Ps 8:6
Matt 28:18
Eph 1:22
Heb 2:8
1 Pet 3:22

15:28
1 Cor 3:23
Phil 3:21

15:24 Greek *every ruler and every authority and power.*   **15:27** Ps 8:6.

15:10 Paul wrote of working harder than the other apostles. This was not an arrogant boast, because he knew that his power came from God and that it really didn't matter who worked hardest. Because of his prominent position as a Pharisee, Paul's conversion made him the object of even greater persecution than the other apostles; thus, he had to work harder to preach the same message.

• **15:12ff** Most Greeks did not believe that people's bodies would be resurrected after death. They saw the afterlife as something that happened only to Greek philosophers, the soul was the real person, imprisoned in a physical body, and at death the soul was released. There was no immortality for the body, but the soul entered an eternal state. Christianity, by contrast, affirms that the body and soul will be united after resurrection. The church at Corinth was in the heart of Greek culture. Thus, many believers had a difficult time believing in a bodily resurrection. Paul wrote this part of his letter to clear up this confusion about the resurrection.

• **15:13-18** The resurrection of Christ is the center of the gospel message. Because Christ rose from the dead as he promised, we know that what he said is true—he is God. Because he rose, we have certainty that our sins are forgiven. Because he rose, he lives and represents us to God. Because he rose and defeated death, we know we will also be raised.

• **15:19** Why does Paul say believers would be miserable if there were only earthly value to Christianity? In Paul's day, Christianity often brought a person persecution, ostracism from family, and, in many cases, poverty. There were few tangible

benefits from being a Christian in that society. It was certainly not a step up the social or career ladder. More important is the fact that if Christ had not been resurrected from the dead, Christians would not be forgiven of their sins or have any hope of eternal life.

15:20 Just as the first part of the harvest was brought to the Temple as an offering (Leviticus 23:10ff) so Christ was the first to rise from the dead and never die again. He is our forerunner, the guarantee of our eventual resurrection to eternal life.

15:21 Death came into the world as a result of Adam and Eve's sin. In Romans 5:12-21, Paul explained why Adam's sin brought sin to all people, how death and sin spread to all humans because of this first sin, and the parallel between Adam's death and Christ's death.

15:24-28 This is not a chronological sequence of events, and no specific time for these events is given. Paul's point is that the resurrected Christ will conquer all evil, including death. See Revelation 20:14 for words about the final destruction of death.

15:25-28 Although God the Father and God the Son are equal, each has a special work to do and an area of sovereign control (15:28). Christ is not inferior to the Father, but his work is to defeat all evil on earth. First, he defeated sin and death on the cross, and in the end he will defeat Satan and all evil. World events may seem out of control, and justice may seem to have vanished. But God is in control, allowing evil to remain for a time until he sends Jesus to earth again. Then he will present to God a perfect new world.

God, so that God, who gave his Son authority over all things, will be utterly supreme over everything everywhere. ²⁹If the dead will not be raised, then what point is there in people being baptized for those who are dead? Why do it unless the dead will someday rise again?

³⁰And why should we ourselves be continually risking our lives, facing death hour by hour? ³¹For I swear, dear brothers and sisters, I face death daily. This is as certain as my pride in what the Lord Jesus Christ has done in you. ³²And what value was there in fighting wild beasts—those men of Ephesus*—if there will be no resurrection from the dead? If there is no resurrection,

"Let's feast and get drunk,
    for tomorrow we die!"*

³³Don't be fooled by those who say such things, for "bad company corrupts good character." ³⁴Come to your senses and stop sinning. For to your shame I say that some of you don't even know God.

The Resurrection Body

³⁵But someone may ask, "How will the dead be raised? What kind of bodies will they have?" ³⁶What a foolish question! When you put a seed into the ground, it doesn't grow into a plant unless it dies first. ³⁷And what you put in the ground is not the plant that will grow, but only a dry little seed of wheat or whatever it is you are planting. ³⁸Then God gives it a new body—just the kind he wants it to have. A different kind of plant grows from each kind of seed. ³⁹And just as there are different kinds of seeds and plants, so also there are different kinds of flesh—whether of humans, animals, birds, or fish.

⁴⁰There are bodies in the heavens, and there are bodies on earth. The glory of the heavenly bodies is different from the beauty of the earthly bodies. ⁴¹The sun has one

15:32a Greek *fighting wild beasts in Ephesus.*   15:32b Isa 22:13.

Marginal references:
15:30 Rom 8:36; 2 Cor 11:26
15:31 2 Cor 4:10-11
15:32 †Isa 22:13; Luke 12:19-21; 2 Cor 1:8
15:34 1 Cor 6:5; Eph 5:14
15:35 Ezek 37:3
15:36 John 12:24
15:38 Gen 1:11

PHYSICAL AND RESURRECTION BODIES

Physical Bodies	Resurrection Bodies
Perishable	Imperishable
Sown in dishonor	Raised in glory
Sown in weakness	Raised in power
Natural	Spiritual
From the dust	From heaven

We all have a body—each looks different; each has different strengths and weaknesses. But as physical, earthly bodies, they are all alike. All believers are promised life after death and a body like Christ's (15:49), a resurrection body.

15:29 Some believers were baptized on behalf of others who had died unbaptized. Nothing more is known about this practice, but it obviously affirms a belief in the resurrection. Paul is not promoting baptism for the dead; he is illustrating his argument that the resurrection is a reality.

• **15:30-34** If death ended it all, enjoying the moment would be all that mattered. But Christians know that there is life beyond the grave and that our life on earth is only a preparation for our life that will never end. What you do today matters for eternity. In light of eternity, sin is a foolish gamble.

15:31, 32 "I face death daily" refers to the dangers Paul encountered daily. The "wild beasts" in Ephesus referred to the savage opposition he had faced there.

15:33 Keeping company with those who deny the resurrection can corrupt good Christian character. Don't let your relationships with unbelievers lead you away from Christ or cause your faith to waver.

15:35ff Paul launches into a discussion about what our resurrected bodies will be like. If you could select your own body, what kind would you choose—strong, athletic, beautiful? Paul explains that we will be recognizable in our resurrected body, yet it will be better than we can imagine, for it will be made to live forever. We will still have our own personality and individuality, but these will be perfected through Christ's work. The Bible does not reveal everything that our resurrected body will be able to do, but we know it will be perfect, without any infirmities (see Philippians 3:21).

• **15:35ff** Paul compares the resurrection with the growth of a seed in a garden. Seeds placed in the ground don't grow unless they "die" first. The plant that grows looks very different from the seed because God gives it a new "body." There are different kinds of bodies—people, animals, fish, birds. Even the angels in heaven have bodies that are different in beauty and glory. Our resurrected body will be very different from our earthly body. It will be a spiritual body full of glory.

kind of glory, while the moon and stars each have another kind. And even the stars differ from each other in their beauty and brightness.

⁴² It is the same way for the resurrection of the dead. Our earthly bodies, which die and decay, will be different when they are resurrected, for they will never die. ⁴³ Our bodies now disappoint us, but when they are raised, they will be full of glory. They are weak now, but when they are raised, they will be full of power. ⁴⁴ They are natural human bodies now, but when they are raised, they will be spiritual bodies. For just as there are natural bodies, so also there are spiritual bodies.

⁴⁵ The Scriptures tell us, "The first man, Adam, became a living person."* But the last Adam—that is, Christ—is a life-giving Spirit. ⁴⁶ What came first was the natural body, then the spiritual body comes later. ⁴⁷ Adam, the first man, was made from the dust of the earth, while Christ, the second man, came from heaven. ⁴⁸ Every human being has an earthly body just like Adam's, but our heavenly bodies will be just like Christ's. ⁴⁹ Just as we are now like Adam, the man of the earth, so we will someday be like Christ, the man from heaven.

⁵⁰ What I am saying, dear brothers and sisters, is that flesh and blood cannot inherit the Kingdom of God. These perishable bodies of ours are not able to live forever.

⁵¹ But let me tell you a wonderful secret God has revealed to us. Not all of us will die, but we will all be transformed. ⁵² It will happen in a moment, in the blinking of an eye, when the last trumpet is blown. For when the trumpet sounds, the Christians who have died* will be raised with transformed bodies. And then we who are living will be transformed so that we will never die. ⁵³ For our perishable earthly bodies must be transformed into heavenly bodies that will never die.

⁵⁴ When this happens—when our perishable earthly bodies have been transformed into heavenly bodies that will never die—then at last the Scriptures will come true:

"Death is swallowed up in victory.*
⁵⁵ O death, where is your victory?
O death, where is your sting?"*

⁵⁶ For sin is the sting that results in death, and the law gives sin its power. ⁵⁷ How we thank God, who gives us victory over sin and death through Jesus Christ our Lord!

⁵⁸ So, my dear brothers and sisters, be strong and steady, always enthusiastic about the Lord's work, for you know that nothing you do for the Lord is ever useless.

15:45 Gen 2:7.   15:52 Greek *the dead*.   15:54 Isa 25:8.   15:55 Hos 13:14.

15:42
Dan 12:3
Matt 13:43
1 Cor 15:50

15:43
Phil 3:20-21
Col 3:4

15:45
†Gen 2:7
John 5:21; 6:63
Rom 8:2
2 Cor 3:17

15:47
Gen 2:7; 3:19
John 3:13, 31

15:48
Phil 3:20-21

15:49
Gen 5:3
Rom 8:29

15:50
John 3:3, 5

15:51
2 Cor 5:2-4
Phil 3:21
1 Thes 4:15-17

15:52
Matt 24:31

15:53
2 Cor 5:4

15:54
†Isa 25:8

15:55
†Hos 13:14

15:56
Rom 4:15; 5:12

15:57
Rom 8:37
1 Jn 5:4

15:58
Rev 14:13

• **15:42-44** Our present body is perishable and prone to decay. Our resurrection body will be transformed. These spiritual body will not be limited by the laws of nature. This does not necessarily mean we'll be superpeople, but our body will be different from and more capable than our present earthly body. Our spiritual body will not be weak, will never get sick, and will never die.

• **15:45** Because Christ rose from the dead, he is a life-giving spirit. This means that he entered into a new form of existence. He is the source of the spiritual life that will result in our resurrection. Christ's new glorified human body now suits his new glorified life—just as Adam's human body was suitable to his natural life. When we are resurrected, God will give us a transformed, eternal body suited to our new eternal life.

15:50-53 We all face limitations. Some may have physical, mental, or emotional disabilities. Some may be blind, but they can see a new way to live. Some may be deaf, but they can hear God's Good News. Some may be lame, but they can walk in God's love. In addition, they have the encouragement that those disabilities are only temporary. Paul tells us that we all will be given new bodies when Christ returns and that these bodies will be without disabilities, never to die or become sick. This can give us hope in our suffering.

15:51, 52 Christians alive at that day will not have to die but will be transformed immediately. A trumpet blast will usher in the new heaven and earth. The Jews would understand the significance of this because trumpets were always blown to signal the start of great festivals and other extraordinary events (Numbers 10:10).

15:54-56 Satan seemed to be victorious in the Garden of Eden (Genesis 3) and at the cross of Jesus. But God turned Satan's apparent victory into defeat when Jesus Christ rose from the dead (Colossians 2:15; Hebrews 2:14, 15). Thus, death is no longer a source of dread or fear. Christ overcame it, and one day we will also. The law will no longer make sinners out of us who cannot keep it. Death has been defeated, and we have hope beyond the grave.

• **15:58** Paul says that because of the resurrection, nothing we do is useless. Sometimes we become apathetic about serving the Lord because we don't see any results. Knowing that Christ has won the ultimate victory should affect the way we live right now. Don't let discouragement over an apparent lack of results keep you from doing the work of the Lord enthusiastically as you have opportunity.

The Collection for Jerusalem

16:1
Acts 11:29; 24:17
Rom 15:25-26
2 Cor 8:9
Gal 2:10

16:2
Acts 20:7

16:3
2 Cor 3:1; 8:18-19

16 Now about the money being collected for the Christians in Jerusalem: You should follow the same procedures I gave to the churches in Galatia. ²On every Lord's Day,* each of you should put aside some amount of money in relation to what you have earned and save it for this offering. Don't wait until I get there and then try to collect it all at once. ³When I come I will write letters of recommendation for the messengers you choose to deliver your gift to Jerusalem. ⁴And if it seems appropriate for me also to go along, then we can travel together.

Paul's Final Instructions

16:5
Acts 19:21
1 Cor 4:19

16:6
Rom 15:24
Titus 3:13

16:7
Acts 18:21

16:8
Acts 2:1; 18:19

16:9
Acts 14:27; 19:8-10
2 Cor 2:12

16:10
Acts 16:1

16:11
1 Tim 4:12

16:12
Acts 18:24
1 Cor 1:12

16:13
Eph 6:10
Phil 1:27; 4:1
1 Thes 3:8

16:14
1 Cor 14:1

16:15
1 Cor 1:16

16:16
1 Thes 5:12

⁵I am coming to visit you after I have been to Macedonia, for I am planning to travel through Macedonia. ⁶It could be that I will stay awhile with you, perhaps all winter, and then you can send me on my way to the next destination. ⁷This time I don't want to make just a short visit and then go right on. I want to come and stay awhile, if the Lord will let me. ⁸In the meantime, I will be staying here at Ephesus until the Festival of Pentecost, ⁹for there is a wide-open door for a great work here, and many people are responding. But there are many who oppose me.

¹⁰When Timothy comes, treat him with respect. He is doing the Lord's work, just as I am. ¹¹Don't let anyone despise him. Send him on his way with your blessings when he returns to me. I am looking forward to seeing him soon, along with the other brothers.

¹²Now about our brother Apollos—I urged him to join the other brothers when they visit you, but he was not willing to come right now. He will be seeing you later, when the time is right.

¹³Be on guard. Stand true to what you believe. Be courageous. Be strong. ¹⁴And everything you do must be done with love.

¹⁵You know that Stephanas and his household were the first to become Christians in Greece,* and they are spending their lives in service to other Christians. I urge you, dear brothers and sisters,* ¹⁶to respect them fully and others like them who serve with such real devotion. ¹⁷I am so glad that Stephanas, Fortunatus, and Achaicus have come here. They have been making up for the help you weren't here to give me. ¹⁸They have been a wonderful encouragement to me, as they have been to you, too. You must give proper honor to all who serve so well.

Paul's Final Greetings

16:19
Rom 16:5

¹⁹The churches here in the province of Asia* greet you heartily in the Lord, along with Aquila and Priscilla and all the others who gather in their home for church meetings.

16:2 Greek *every first day of the week.*   **16:15a** Greek *were the firstfruits in Achaia,* the southern region of the Greek peninsula.   **16:15b** Greek *brothers;* also in 16:20.   **16:19** *Asia* was a Roman province in what is now western Turkey.

16:1ff Paul had just said that no good deed is ever useless (15:58). In this chapter he mentions some practical deeds that have value for all Christians.

• **16:1-4** The Christians in Jerusalem were suffering from poverty and famine, so Paul was collecting money for them (Romans 15:25-31; 2 Corinthians 8:4; 9:1ff). He suggested that believers set aside a certain amount each week and give it to the church until he arrived to take it on to Jerusalem. Paul had planned to go straight to Corinth from Ephesus, but he changed his mind (2 Corinthians 1; 2). When he finally arrived, he took the gift and delivered it to the Jerusalem church (Acts 21:18; 24:17).

16:10, 11 Paul was sending Timothy ahead to Corinth. Paul respected Timothy and had worked closely with him (Philippians 2:22; 1 Timothy 1:2). Although Timothy was young, Paul encouraged the Corinthian church to welcome him because he was doing the Lord's work. God's work is not limited by age. Paul wrote two personal letters to Timothy that have been preserved in the Bible (1 and 2 Timothy).

16:12 Apollos, who had preached in Corinth, was doing evangelistic work in Greece (see Acts 18:24-28; 1 Corinthians 3:3ff). Apollos didn't go to Corinth right away, partly because he knew of the factions there and didn't want to cause any more divisions.

• **16:13, 14** As the Corinthians awaited Paul's next visit, they were directed to (1) be on their guard against spiritual dangers, (2) stand firm in the faith, (3) be courageous, (4) be strong, and (5) do everything with kindness and in love. Today, as we wait for the return of Christ, we should follow the same instructions.

• **16:19** Aquila and Priscilla were tentmakers (or leatherworkers) whom Paul had met in Corinth (Acts 18:1-3). They followed Paul to Ephesus and lived there with him, helping to teach others about Jesus (Romans 16:3-5). Many in the Corinthian church would have known this Christian couple. They are also mentioned in Acts 18:18, 26; Romans 16:3; and 2 Timothy 4:19.

²⁰ All the brothers and sisters here have asked me to greet you for them. Greet each other in Christian love.*

²¹ Here is my greeting, which I write with my own hand—PAUL.

²² If anyone does not love the Lord, that person is cursed. Our Lord, come!*

²³ May the grace of the Lord Jesus be with you.

²⁴ My love to all of you in Christ Jesus.*

16:20 Greek *with a sacred kiss.*   **16:22** From Aramaic, *Marana tha.*   **16:24** Some manuscripts add *Amen.*

16:20
Rom 16:16

16:21
Gal 6:11
Col 4:18
2 Thes 3:17
Phlm 1:19

16:22
Gal 1:8-9

16:21 Paul had a helper, or secretary, who wrote down this letter while he dictated. Paul wrote the final words, however, in his own handwriting. This is similar to adding a handwritten postscript (P.S.) to a typewritten letter. It also served to verify that this was a genuine letter from the apostle and not a forgery.

• **16:22** The Lord Jesus Christ is coming back to earth again. To Paul, this was a wonderful hope, the very best he could look forward to. He was not afraid of seeing Christ—he could hardly wait! Do you share Paul's eager anticipation? Those who love Christ are looking forward to that glorious time of his return (Titus 2:13). To those who do not love the Lord, however, Paul says, let them be cursed.

• **16:24** The church at Corinth was a church in trouble. Paul lovingly and forcefully confronted them and pointed them back to Christ. He dealt with divisions and conflicts, selfishness, inconsiderate use of freedom, disorder in worship, misuse of spiritual gifts, and wrong attitudes about the resurrection.

In every church, there are problems that create tensions and divisions. We should not ignore or gloss over problems in our churches or in our life. Instead, like Paul, we should deal with problems head-on as they arise. The lesson for us in 1 Corinthians is that unity and love in a church are far more important than leaders and labels.

STUDY QUESTIONS

Thirteen lessons for individual or group study

It's always exciting to get more than you expect. And that's what you'll find in this Bible study guide—much more than you expect. Our goal was to write thoughtful, practical, dependable, and application-oriented studies of God's Word.

This study guide contains the complete text of the selected Bible book. The commentary is accurate, complete, and loaded with unique charts, maps, and profiles of Bible people.

With the Bible text, extensive notes and helps, and questions to guide discussion, these Life Application Study Guides have everything you need in one place.

The lessons in this Bible study guide will work for large classes as well as small-group studies. To get everyone involved in your discussions, encourage participants to answer the questions before each meeting.

Each lesson is divided into five easy-to-lead sections. The section called "Reflect" introduces you and the members of your group to a specific area of life touched by the lesson. "Read" shows which chapters to read and which notes and other features to use. Additional questions help you understand the passage. "Realize" brings into focus the biblical principle to be learned with questions, a special insight, or both. "Respond" helps you make connections with your own situation and personal needs. The questions are designed to help you find areas in your life where you can apply the biblical truths. "Resolve" helps you map out action plans for that day.

Begin and end each lesson with prayer, asking for the Holy Spirit's guidance, direction, and wisdom.

Recommended time allotments for each section of a lesson are as follows:

Segment	60 minutes	90 minutes
Reflect on your life	5 minutes	10 minutes
Read the passage	10 minutes	15 minutes
Realize the principle	15 minutes	20 minutes
Respond to the message	20 minutes	30 minutes
Resolve to take action	10 minutes	15 minutes

All five sections work together to help a person learn the lessons, live out the principles, and obey the commands taught in the Bible.

Also, at the end of each lesson, there is a section entitled, "More for studying other themes in this section." These questions will help you lead the group in studying other parts of each section not covered in depth by the main lesson.

And remember, it is a message to obey, not just to listen to. If you don't obey, you are only fooling yourself. For if you just listen and don't obey, it is like looking at your face in a mirror but doing nothing to improve your appearance. You see yourself, walk away, and forget what you look like. But if you keep looking steadily into God's perfect law—the law that sets you free—and if you do what it says and don't forget what you heard, then God will bless you for doing it. (James 1:22–25)

LESSON 1
LIGHT AT THE END OF THE TUNNEL
1 CORINTHIANS 1:1–9

REFLECT
on your life

1 What's the best church you ever attended? What made it such a good church?

_____
_____
_____
_____
_____

2 What were some of the problems this church faced?

_____
_____
_____
_____
_____

READ
the passage

Read the Introduction to 1 Corinthians, the map "Corinth and Ephesus" (chapter 1), 1 Corinthians 1:1–9, and the following notes:

❏ 1:1 ❏ 1:2 ❏ 1:3 ❏ 1:7 ❏ 1:7–9

3 Why did Paul write this letter to the church in Corinth?

_____
_____
_____
_____

4 What was the city of Corinth like?

_____

_____

_____

_____

5 Why did Paul begin his letter with such a positive opening?

_____

_____

_____

_____

_____

6 List five problems that Paul wrote about in 1 Corinthians. Which of these are of interest to you?

_____

_____

_____

_____

_____

7 Paul reminded the Corinthians of what God had done for them in the past (1:4–9). What are the benefits of remembering God's work in your life and in the life of your church?

_____

REALIZE
the principle

_____

_____

_____

The first-century church was far from ideal, especially in Corinth. Pressured by a pagan culture, the Christians there were divided by conflicts and immorality. Though the church at Corinth was gifted, it was spiritually immature. In many ways, it was like some young churches today. Problems brought discouragement. Paul wrote to this church to bring them hope and to confront the problems plaguing them. They needed to change, and God was able to help them. Paul's letter to the Corinthians will encourage us, too, whether our problems are at church or at home.

8 What problems do churches today have that are similar to those faced by the
Corinthian church in the first century?

_____

_____

_____

_____

_____

_____

_____

9 What problems do churches encounter today that they did not face in the past?

_____

_____

_____

_____

_____

_____

_____

RESPOND
to the message

10 If Paul were to write a letter to your church, what might he commend?

_____

_____

_____

_____

_____

_____

11 What would he want to correct?

_____

_____

_____

_____

_____

12 What can you do about the problems confronting your church?

_____

_____

_____

_____

_____

13 Pray each day this week for your church. Ask God what you can do to help strengthen your church. What church leaders, members, and attenders can you pray for this week?

RESOLVE
to take action

_____

_____

_____

_____

_____

_____

A Besides the Corinthians, to whom does this letter apply (1:2)? Which needs of the Corinthian church are also needs in your church?

MORE
for studying
other themes
in this section

B What were some of the good qualities of the Corinthian church (1:2–9)? Where did they get these qualities? What good qualities does your church have?

C Why did the Corinthians "eagerly wait for the return of our Lord Jesus Christ" (1:7)? What does this mean for you? How does it apply to your responsibilities and commitments?

D What could the Corinthian Christians count on (1:8, 9)? How might this assurance affect a Christian? How does it affect you?

LESSON 2
FOOLISH WISDOM
1 CORINTHIANS 1:10—2:16

REFLECT
on your life

1 List two or three common wise sayings or aphorisms (for example, "A penny saved is a penny earned").

_____

_____

_____

_____

2 What is your favorite wise saying?

_____

_____

_____

_____

READ
the passage

Read 1 Corinthians 1:10—2:16 and the following notes:

❒ 1:19   ❒ 1:22–24   ❒ 1:25   ❒ 2:4   ❒ 2:7   ❒ 2:10   ❒ 2:14, 15

3 What is foolish about the message of the cross (1:18–28)?

_____

_____

_____

_____

4 Why has God chosen what the world considers foolish (1:27–31)?

_____

_____

_____

_____

_____

5 How were the Corinthians thinking with the world's mind and not with the mind of Christ?

_____

_____

_____

_____

_____

6 For what reasons do many people today consider the message of the cross to be foolish?

_____

REALIZE
the principle

_____

_____

_____

_____

Conventional wisdom says that changing the world requires eloquent spokespersons, popular leaders, and the use of power. Instead, God used ordinary, humble, and powerless people. And most amazing of all, he used the cross. Who would expect a Savior to die as a criminal? No wonder God's ways seem foolish to the world. The problem in the Corinthian church was that people were still looking at life from the world's perspective. This led to popularity contests, divisions, and spiritual pride. Paul had to bring them back to reality.

7 Why is it important to live God's way rather than the world's?

_____

_____

_____

_____

8 Why doesn't the world understand God's ways?

_____

_____

_____

_____

9 What are some examples of God's values that conflict with your culture's values?

_____

_____

_____

_____

_____

10 Why is it difficult to live by God's wisdom and reject the world's wisdom?

_____

_____

_____

_____

RESPOND
to the message

11 How are Christians tempted to embrace the world's values?

_____

_____

_____

_____

_____

12 Where in your own life does this battle occur?

_____

_____

_____

_____

13 How do you tell the difference between God's wisdom and the world's wisdom?

_____

_____

_____

14 Write down at least one area in your life in which you have been listening to the world more than God.

_____

_____

_____

_____

RESOLVE
to take action

15 How would God's wisdom change your situation?

_____

_____

_____

_____

16 What can you do this week to follow God's wisdom?

_____

_____

_____

_____

A Why does the message of Christ seem foolish to a Jewish person? What unique issues might need to be addressed in explaining the gospel to him or her?

B How did Paul approach ministry (2:1–6)? What lessons can those in ministry today learn from Paul's approach?

C What does it mean to have the mind of Christ (2:16)? How does Paul's assurance that we have the mind of Christ affect you?

D What is "the secret wisdom of God" (2:7)? How can a person have this wisdom?

MORE
for studying
other themes
in this section

REFLECT
on your life

1 List as many different church denominations as you can think of.

_____

_____

_____

_____

_____

_____

2 How did we end up with so many different kinds of churches?

_____

_____

_____

_____

READ
the passage

Read 1 Corinthians 3:1—4:21 and the following notes:

❐ 3:6   ❐ 3:10, 11   ❐ 3:10–17   ❐ 3:13–15   ❐ 4:1, 2   ❐ 4:6, 7   ❐ 4:15

3 What situation in the church was Paul addressing (3:1–4)?

_____

_____

_____

4 What were some of the reasons for this situation (1:3, 4)?

_____

_____

_____

_____

5 Why was this troubling to Paul (3:1–9)?

_____

_____

_____

_____

6 How did Paul address this problem? (See 3:8–10; 4:6, 7.)

_____

_____

_____

_____

7 Why do you think Paul placed such an emphasis on his lifestyle and apostle-ship in this passage of Scripture?

_____

_____

_____

_____

_____

REALIZE
the principle

Paul spoke to the Corinthians as their spiritual father. He had a pure and genuine concern for their welfare and spiritual growth, but he saw the young church being split into factions according to personalities and leadership styles. Because people were taking such pride in the groups they belonged to, the church was divided. It's good and normal to appreciate gifted people and to follow spiritual leaders, but when that appreciation leads to feelings of superiority, arrogance, or pride, the church is weakened and the Lord is saddened. As you look around at other groups, both inside and outside your church, be appreciative of differences. Thank God if you are in a church where your needs are being met and you are growing in Christ. But remember the simple truth that there is only one foundation, Jesus Christ, and that all we have or do comes from him. Watch out for the natural tendency to take sides.

8 What does it mean that Jesus Christ is the "foundation" (3:11)? How do we build on this foundation?

_____

_____

_____

_____

RESPOND
to the message

9 What kinds of things are "gold, silver, jewels"? What kinds of things are "wood, hay, or straw" (3:12)?

_____

_____

_____

_____

_____

10 In your experience, what are some of the main causes of divisions and splits in churches?

_____

_____

_____

_____

11 When can appreciation for a leader become a problem?

_____

_____

_____

_____

12 In your church, what are some of the potential (or existing) causes of division?

_____

_____

_____

_____

13 What are some ways to promote unity in your church, either to prevent divisions or to help heal the ones that exist?

_____

_____

_____

_____

14 Ask God to use you to promote unity in your church. Write a one- or two-sentence statement that expresses your determination to do so.

_____

RESOLVE
to take action

_____

_____

_____

15 Write down the names of the leaders in your church (or other spiritual leaders you follow) for whom you will pray this week. Ask God to use them and to protect them from the temptations of power and pride.

_____

_____

_____

_____

A Discuss the relationship between faith and deeds in the Christian life. What incentives are found in this passage for being a wise builder? What are you building on the foundation of Jesus Christ?

MORE
for studying
other themes
in this section

B How will we be rewarded in heaven for our obedience and faithfulness (3:8, 13–15)?

C What would it have been like to have been an apostle? How does God call you to similar experiences?

D Why did Paul urge people to live as he lived? How would you want people to imitate you?

REFLECT
on your life

1 What kinds of disciplinary methods did your parents use on you when you were a child?

_____

_____

_____

2 What disciplinary methods did they use when you were in high school?

_____

_____

_____

3 What is the purpose of discipline?

_____

_____

_____

_____

READ
the passage

Read 1 Corinthians 5:1—6:20, the chart "Church Discipline," and the following notes:

❑ 5:1ff   ❑ 5:5   ❑ 5:6   ❑ 5:10, 11   ❑ 5:12   ❑ 6:1–6   ❑ 6:9–11   ❑ 6:12, 13

❑ 6:13   ❑ 6:19, 20

4 What instructions did Paul give to resolve the immoral situation described in 1 Corinthians 5?

_____

_____

_____

_____

_____

_____

5 What is the purpose of church discipline (5:5)?

_____

_____

_____

_____

6 What does the phrase "cast this man out of the church and into Satan's hands" mean (5:5)?

_____

_____

_____

_____

_____

People sometimes think of church discipline as negative and unloving. But when applied as the Bible describes, it can be an instrument of healing and forgiveness. Paul taught the Corinthian believers to use discipline to keep the church pure and to bring wayward members back to Christ. We need such discipline because it is easy to gloss over sin in our life and in the church. Sin needs to be dealt with so it will not gain a foothold.

REALIZE
the principle

7 Why is purity such a vital issue for a Christian and for the church?

_____

_____

_____

_____

8 What role does church discipline have in the Christian's call to purity?

_____

_____

_____

_____

_____

9 Since each Christian struggles with sin every day, when is church discipline appropriate?

_____

_____

_____

_____

_____

_____

RESPOND
to the message

10 How would you feel if someone approached you with a rebuke or a correction? What would be your response?

_____

_____

_____

_____

_____

_____

11 What stages of church discipline can all Christians be a part of? (See the chart "Church Discipline.")

_____

_____

_____

_____

_____

12 How can being accountable to others help a person remain pure?

_____

_____

_____

_____

13 How is it possible to honor God with your body?

_____

_____

_____

_____

14 Who knows you well enough to hold you accountable for a lifestyle of purity? When could you talk to that person about a mutual agreement to pray for each other and be open with each other about purity issues?

_____

RESOLVE
to take action

_____

_____

15 Pray for your church to be a place that encourages and promotes biblical purity.

A Paul gave instructions on lawsuits between Christians (6:1–8). How should Christians settle their disputes? Why is it important for Christians not to go to court against one another? To what extent should a Christian go to avoid taking another Christian to court?

MORE
for studying
other themes
in this section

B What does it mean that our body is the "temple of the Holy Spirit" (6:19)? How does this influence your behavior?

C What is so harmful about sexual immorality? How does our culture make it difficult for people to remain sexually pure? What can we do to counteract those influences?

LESSON 5
SINGLES OR DOUBLES?
1 CORINTHIANS 7:1–40

REFLECT
on your life

1 Give an example of when people might think *The grass is greener on the other side of the fence.*

_____

_____

_____

_____

_____

2 When might married and single people think this way?

_____

_____

_____

_____

READ
the passage

Read 1 Corinthians 7:1–40 and the following notes:

❒ 7:3–11 ❒ 7:4 ❒ 7:7 ❒ 7:12–14 ❒ 7:20 ❒ 7:28

3 What are the different life situations addressed in this chapter (7:1–40)?

_____

_____

_____

_____

4 What are the advantages of remaining single? (See 7:7, 8, 24, 28, 32–34, 36–38.)

_____

_____

_____

_____

5 What are the advantages of being married? (See 7:7, 9, 24, 36–38.)

_____

_____

_____

_____

It is easy to envy what others have. The problem with this is it assumes that what you have is inferior to what you don't have. This is especially true with marriage and singleness. In reality, both have accompanying benefits and problems. Paul saw this in the Corinthian church, where there was tremendous pressure for sexual immorality and a sense of urgency about spreading the gospel. Single people wanted to be married to avoid sin, and married people wanted to have more time to serve God. Both singleness and marriage are gifts, with advantages and disadvantages to each. Both can be used to glorify God. Instead of worrying about what you don't have, thank God for what you have, and focus on serving God where you are.

REALIZE
the principle

6 What do married people today envy about singleness?

_____

_____

_____

_____

7 What do single people today envy about marriage?

_____

_____

_____

_____

8 What are some of the reasons that marriage is to be entered into with care and much prayer?

_____

_____

_____

_____

RESPOND
to the message

9 Why is it difficult to remain single in our society?

_____

_____

_____

_____

_____

10 Why is it difficult to remain married in our society?

_____

_____

_____

_____

_____

11 Identify one specific aspect of marriage or singleness that you envy.

_____

_____

_____

_____

12 What makes it difficult for you to be content with your situation?

_____

_____

_____

_____

_____

13 Pray and thank God for your singleness or marriage.

14 What opportunities do you have to use your single or married status to glorify God?

RESOLVE
to take action

_____

_____

_____

_____

_____

_____

A What instructions did Paul give to married couples about their sexual relationship (7:1–5)? Why is it important to take these instructions seriously today?

MORE
for studying
other themes
in this section

B What reasons for divorce does Paul mention? When is divorce inappropriate? What plan of action would you suggest to a Christian who is in an unhappy marriage?

C In what ways are children of a believing parent holy (7:14)? What kind of parenting responsibilities does this imply?

D How do you think the Corinthians understood the phrase "the time that remains is very short" (7:29)? Time is even shorter now. How might this fact affect your lifestyle?

E In what issues other than marriage is it sometimes difficult to be content?

F Based on this chapter, what advice would you give to a young person about to get married?

REFLECT
on your life

1 What personal rights and freedoms have been issues in the news recently?

_____

_____

_____

2 Describe a time when you had to stand up for your rights. How did you feel in that situation?

_____

_____

_____

_____

_____

READ
the passage

Read 1 Corinthians 8:1—9:18, the chart "Stronger, Weaker Believers," and the following notes:

❐ 8:1 ❐ 8:4–9 ❐ 8:10–13 ❐ 9:4ff

3 What was the controversy in Corinth about meat that had been sacrificed to idols (8:1–13)?

_____

_____

_____

_____

4 What limitations did this place on the Corinthians' rights (8:9–13)?

_____

_____

_____

_____

5 What rights could Paul have insisted on (9:4–15)?

_____

_____

_____

_____

_____

6 What was more important to Paul than exercising his rights (9:15–18)?

_____

_____

_____

_____

_____

_____

In our society, people are expected to stand up for their rights and watch out for themselves. God's way is just the opposite. Although we have rights, there are certain values and priorities that take precedence over our rights. These include not hurting a brother or sister in Christ, not causing others to stumble, and, above all, doing what God has called us to do. We are to live with humility and love, placing God and others above ourself.

REALIZE
the principle

7 Although eating food sacrificed to idols wasn't wrong, why did Paul counsel against it?

_____

_____

_____

_____

8 What are some modern-day equivalents of food sacrificed to idols?

_____

_____

_____

_____

_____

_____

_____

RESPOND
to the message

9 Give some examples of how insisting on your rights can cause others to stumble.

_____

_____

_____

_____

_____

10 When would it become necessary to limit your rights?

_____

_____

_____

_____

_____

11 What sensitivities of others would you want to be careful about offending?

_____

_____

_____

_____

_____

12 Whom do you know who might be affected by your freedoms and rights?

_____

_____

RESOLVE
to take action

_____

_____

13 What can you do to help that person grow in his or her faith?

_____

_____

_____

_____

A What advantages and disadvantages can you see to someone providing for his or her own financial support while doing ministry? What can you do to support those in ministry?

B Why was it important for Paul to preach whether he wanted to or not (9:17, 18)? What areas of Christian responsibility are your duty to perform in much the same way?

C In this passage, who are stronger brothers and who are weaker brothers (8:7–13)? What responsibilities does each have toward the other? What responsibilities does this give you?

MORE
for studying
other themes
in this section

REFLECT
on your life

1 Choose one of the following activities, and tell what it would take to be excellent in it: ❏ chess ❏ cooking ❏ research ❏ football ❏ piano ❏ writing ❏ carpentry.

_____

_____

_____

_____

_____

READ
the passage

Read 1 Corinthians 9:19—11:1 and the following notes:

❏ 9:24–27 ❏ 9:27 ❏ 10:1–5 ❏ 10:7–10 ❏ 10:11 ❏ 10:16–21 ❏ 10:21

❏ 10:23, 24 ❏ 10:28–33 ❏ 10:31

2 What made Paul excellent at telling people about Christ (9:19–27)?

_____

_____

_____

_____

3 How did Paul choose his activities? (See 9:23, 27; 10:23, 24, 31.)

_____

_____

_____

_____

4 How did the people of Israel get sidetracked from their goal (10:1–13)?

_____

_____

_____

_____

_____

5 How would you describe Paul's purpose in life?

_____

_____

_____

_____

_____

REALIZE
the principle

Paul was a driven man. He had a clear sense of what was important and moved ahead accordingly. Paul knew that God had called him to share the good news about Christ, so he ordered his life around that purpose. Paul was motivated by the needs of people, his responsibility to use his gifts, and the knowledge that God would evaluate his life. As a result, he was dedicated to telling others about Christ. God has a unique calling and purpose for each of us. To be effective, we need to have a sense of purpose and to know where to focus our energies.

6 How does a person determine God's purpose for his or her life?

_____

_____

_____

_____

7 How does this purpose relate to the nonspiritual areas of life, such as home, school, work, and recreation?

_____

_____

_____

_____

8 How can a person do "all for the glory of God" (10:31)?

RESPOND
to the message

9 If you could accomplish one thing for God during this life, what would it be?

10 What resources (spiritual gifts, relationships, material possessions, time, education) has God given you to accomplish this goal?

11 How can you bring more of your activities into line with God's purpose for your life?

12 What changes do you need to make to become more focused toward God's purpose for your life?

_____

_____

_____

_____

_____

13 What step can you take this week?

_____

_____

_____

_____

A To what does the word *prize* in 1 Corinthians 9:24–27 refer? How can you make this a more effective motivator in your life?

B What was Paul's method for sharing the gospel (9:19–23)? What's the difference between finding "common ground with everyone" (9:22) and unhealthy compromise? How can you find "common ground with everyone" without compromising your commitment to Christ?

C What did Paul mean when he talked about the possibility of being disqualified (9:27)? What might this idea mean for you?

D The Israelites lost sight of their purpose even though God did miracles in their presence (10:3, 4). What might this example mean for you?

E How can a Christian drink both the cup of the Lord and the cup of demons (10:14–22)? How would this be possible in your life?

1 If you went to church as a child, jot down several adjectives that describe what you remember worship services being like.

REFLECT
on your life

_____

_____

_____

_____

2 Describe the ideal worship service today. What should be a part of every good worship service?

_____

_____

_____

_____

_____

_____

Read 1 Corinthians 11:2–34 and the following notes:

❐ 11:2–16   ❐ 11:3   ❐ 11:9–11   ❐ 11:14, 15   ❐ 11:21, 22   ❐ 11:27ff

READ
the passage

❐ 11:27–34

3 How was the issue concerning head coverings affecting the Corinthians' worship (11:2–16)?

_____

_____

_____

_____

4 Describe the problems Paul addressed regarding the Lord's Supper. Why was this such a concern to him (11:17–34)?

_____

_____

_____

5 What do the issues of male/female relationships in worship and proper attitude toward the Lord's Supper have in common?

_____

_____

_____

_____

REALIZE
the principle

The Corinthians brought their problems to worship with them. Some of these problems, such as the matter of head coverings, involved disagreement over how they were being perceived by outsiders. Other problems, such as their abuse of the Lord's Supper, stemmed from broken relationships, pride, and self-centeredness. Paul wanted them to know that the attitudes they brought to worship and the way they acted during worship had great importance. In worship we come into God's presence and declare that we are his people, united together in faith. We can't do that if we are divided, fighting, or jockeying for the best seats. We must come into God's presence focused on him and unified as a group. We must worship with respect toward one another and toward God. Otherwise, we miss the purpose of coming together in the first place.

6 What conflicts and problems prevent churches from worshiping well?

_____

_____

_____

_____

_____

7 How would you evaluate a worship service at your church?

_____

_____

_____

_____

RESPOND
to the message

8 What preoccupations sometimes hinder you from coming to worship services properly prepared?

_____

_____

_____

_____

_____

9 What could you do to eliminate those hindrances?

_____

_____

_____

_____

10 How might you improve the quality of your church's worship services?

_____

_____

_____

_____

11 How can you prepare yourself to receive the Lord's Supper?

_____

_____

_____

_____

RESOLVE
to take action

12 What are one or two things you can do on Saturday nights or Sunday mornings to prepare for worship?

_____

_____

_____

_____

13 What is one thing you can do to enhance the worship experience of your family or of those around you?

_____

_____

_____

_____

_____

A What does your church believe about the role of women in the church today? What changes would enable all people to participate in the life of the church?

B The Corinthians had to be careful about head coverings because of what such coverings meant to some people in their culture. What cultural practices should Christians be careful about today because of what they mean to others?

C Some people were "weak and sick," and some had "even died" because they abused the Lord's Supper (11:30). What does it mean to partake of the Lord's Supper unworthily?

MORE
for studying
other themes
in this section

LESSON 9
BODY BUILDERS
1 CORINTHIANS 12:1–31

REFLECT
on your life

1 What parts of your body are involved in changing a lightbulb?

_____

_____

_____

_____

_____

2 Recall a time when you stubbed your toe. How did the injury affect your entire body?

_____

_____

_____

_____

_____

READ
the passage

Read 1 Corinthians 12:1–31 and the following notes:

❐ 12:12   ❐ 12:13   ❐ 12:14–24   ❐ 12:25, 26

3 How is the church like a human body (12:12–26)?

_____

_____

_____

_____

_____

4 When does this body function at its best (12:12–26)?

_____

_____

_____

_____

_____

The Christians at Corinth thought some spiritual gifts were more important than others. They thought that some Christians had highly important gifts, while others did not. God wanted them to know that he gives *every* Christian a vital function. None of us is small and unnecessary in God's kingdom. Each person has something vital to contribute. There are no unimportant or unnecessary people in the body of Christ because God has given each of us valuable gifts and abilities "as a means of helping the entire church" (12:7).

REALIZE
the principle

5 What causes us to value some gifts in the church more than others?

_____

_____

_____

_____

6 How can you tell when a church values all gifts equally?

_____

_____

_____

_____

_____

7 What reasons do people have for not using their gifts for God's service?

_____

_____

RESPOND
to the message

_____

_____

_____

8 What gifts or roles in your church tend to be overlooked, unappreciated, or unrecognized?

_____

_____

_____

_____

9 What can be done to show appreciation for people whose gifts are usually overlooked?

_____

_____

_____

_____

10 How does a person discover what his or her role in the church might be?

_____

_____

_____

_____

11 What gifts do you have that God wants you to use in the body of Christ?

_____

_____

_____

_____

_____

RESOLVE
to take action

12 Whom can you commend this week for using their gifts in God's service? (Try to think of people whose gifts aren't ordinarily recognized.)

_____

_____

_____

_____

13 What is one way you can use your unique gift(s) to serve the body of Christ this week?

_____

_____

_____

_____

_____

A Christians must be careful not to follow false teachers (12:1–3). How can a person avoid being deceived by false teachers?

MORE
for studying
other themes
in this section

B What is a local church? What difference can a local church make in its community?

C What is the purpose of spiritual gifts (12:7)? How have you been able to use your gifts for this purpose?

D What are the "most helpful gifts" (12:31)? If you do not have one of these gifts, how can you use the gifts you have to help those whose gifts are "most helpful"?

LESSON 10
LOVELINESS
1 CORINTHIANS 13:1–13

REFLECT
on your life

1 Who was your first childhood "love"?

_____

_____

_____

2 How has your understanding of love changed since then?

_____

_____

_____

_____

_____

_____

READ
the passage

Read 1 Corinthians 13:1–13 and the following notes:

❐ 13:1ff ❐ 13:4–7 ❐ 13:12 ❐ 13:13

3 What good things can be used or seen as a substitute for love (13:1–3)?

_____

_____

_____

_____

4 Why is love so important (13:1–3)?

_____

_____

_____

_____

5 What symptoms show that love is missing in the life of a believer (13:4–8)?

_____

_____

_____

_____

6 What feature of love sets it apart from all the spiritual gifts (13:8–12)?

_____

_____

_____

_____

The Corinthian believers were very gifted people (1:7). In fact, they had impressive gifts, such as prophecy, tongues, and faith. But the Corinthians were unloving in the way they treated each other and took pride in their gifts. They lived as if spiritual gifts were more important than love. But Paul pointed out that love is most important of all. No matter what your talents and abilities, what really matters to God is whether you demonstrate love toward others.

REALIZE
the principle

7 How would you summarize the description of love in this chapter?

_____

_____

_____

8 How has God demonstrated this kind of love?

_____

_____

_____

_____

9 What makes it difficult for us to love this way?

_____

_____

_____

_____

_____

10 How can Christians find the motivation and strength to love as they should?

_____

_____

_____

_____

11 Many people talk about love, but there seem to be few loving people. What often takes the place of love in our society?

_____

_____

_____

_____

RESPOND
to the message

12 In the spirit of 1 Corinthians 13:1–3, fill in the blank with a talent or ability you have: "If I have the gift of _____, without love I would be no good to anybody."

13 How could this gift be used in an unloving way?

_____

_____

_____

14 How could you exercise this gift in a loving way?

_____

_____

_____

_____

15 When is it difficult for you to act in love toward someone close to you?

_____

_____

_____

16 What will it take for you to be more consistently loving toward others?

_____

_____

_____

_____

17 Think of one relationship in which you need to demonstrate love. How do your actions toward this person need to change?

_____

_____

_____

_____

RESOLVE
to take action

18 What will you do for this person in the coming week?

_____

_____

_____

_____

A When will we no longer need spiritual gifts (13:9, 10)? How should we use them in the meantime? Who could benefit from the use of your gifts?

B What is hopeful about the future for Christians (13:8–12)? What about this encourages you? How can your life reflect this hope now?

MORE
for studying
other themes
in this section

REFLECT
on your life

1 What spiritual gifts are used in a typical Sunday morning worship service at your church?

_____

_____

_____

_____

_____

2 What gifts did you use last Sunday at church during worship?

_____

_____

_____

_____

_____

READ
the passage

Read 1 Corinthians 14:1–40 and the following notes:

❏ 14:1   ❏ 14:2   ❏ 14:22–25   ❏ 14:26ff   ❏ 14:33

3 What kinds of gifts should believers desire (14:1, 13, 39)?

_____

_____

_____

_____

4 How should all gifts be used? (See 14:2–12, 26–32, 38, 39.)

_____

_____

_____

_____

5 In what ways should we limit our use of spiritual gifts? (See 14:13–19, 27–32.)

_____

_____

_____

_____

_____

6 What is the relationship between the way we worship and the purpose of worship?

_____

_____

_____

_____

REALIZE
the principle

All of our spiritual gifts, talents, and abilities are given to us by God for the benefit of others. Our spiritual gifts are specifically for building up our brothers and
sisters in Christ. God expects us to use them for this purpose. Because the
believers in Corinth were spiritually immature, they were using their gifts to help
themselves rather than others. As a result, when they gathered together for worship, they were divided rather than unified. God wants us to use our spiritual
gifts to help and build up his people. Instead of expecting people to give to you,
or focusing your gifts on yourself, use God's gifts to benefit others.

7 How does a believer's spiritual maturity affect the way he or she uses spiritual
gifts in worship?

_____

_____

_____

_____

_____

8 This chapter is linked to the previous chapter with the statement, "Let love be your highest goal, but also desire the special abilities the Spirit gives" (14:1). How are love and spiritual gifts related?

_____

_____

_____

_____

_____

_____

RESPOND
to the message

9 What opportunities do people in your church have to discover their gifts and put them into practice?

_____

_____

_____

_____

_____

10 What are some ways you can make sure that worship in your church is "done properly and in order" (14:40)?

_____

_____

_____

_____

_____

RESOLVE
to take action

11 How can you use your spiritual gifts to enhance worship and help others?

_____

_____

_____

_____

12 What spiritual leader in your church could help you find a way to use your gifts in the church?

_____

_____

_____

_____

_____

A What does it mean for women to be silent in the church? What is the role of women in your church? How does your church interpret these passages and make a place for women to use their spiritual gifts?

B What is the function of prophecy in the New Testament? How does it compare to Old Testament prophecy? If you have the gift of prophecy, how can you exercise it responsibly in your church?

MORE
for studying
other themes
in this section

REFLECT
on your life

1 What is heaven like?

_____

_____

_____

_____

2 What about heaven are you looking forward to? What are you apprehensive about?

_____

_____

_____

_____

READ
the passage

Read 1 Corinthians 15:1–58, the chart "Physical and Resurrection Bodies" (chapter 15), and the following notes:

❏ 15:5–8   ❏ 15:12ff   ❏ 15:13–18   ❏ 15:19   ❏ 15:30–34   ❏ 15:35ff

❏ 15:42–44   ❏ 15:45   ❏ 15:58

3 Why is it so important to the Christian faith that Jesus Christ rose physically from the grave (15:12–19)?

_____

_____

_____

4 What would be the implications for our faith if the Resurrection were a hoax (15:17–19)?

_____

_____

_____

_____

5 When will death finally be defeated (15:20–28)?

_____

_____

_____

_____

6 What will our resurrected bodies be like (15:35–49)?

_____

_____

_____

7 How should belief in the resurrection of Christ influence how a Christian lives?

_____

_____

_____

_____

REALIZE
the principle

Nothing is more important to the Christian faith than the truth of the resurrection of Jesus. Because Jesus was actually raised physically, all believers will be raised to eternal glory as well. This isn't just a theoretical doctrine for Christians to discuss. Christ's resurrection puts everything in a new perspective. Life and death, work and recreation, values and priorities—all look different when viewed in light of the resurrection that is to come. Because Christ lives, you can live now with confidence in God and hope for the future.

8 What is the evidence for the resurrection of Jesus?

_____

_____

_____

9 Why does the truth of Christ's resurrection give Christians hope?

_____

_____

_____

_____

_____

_____

10 What do you think would cause people to deny the resurrection of Christ?

_____

_____

_____

_____

_____

_____

RESPOND
to the message

11 In what situations would you use the story of Jesus' resurrection to give someone hope?

_____

_____

_____

_____

_____

_____

12 How would you answer someone who says that the resurrection of Christ is just a matter of faith?

_____

_____

_____

_____

_____

_____

13 What changes would occur in your life if you began to live more fully in light of the resurrection to come?

_____

_____

_____

_____

_____

_____

14 As a Christian, you have a reason for hope. How does this hope affect the way you live?

_____

RESOLVE
to take action

_____

_____

_____

_____

15 In what situations can belief in the Resurrection give you comfort and hope?

_____

_____

_____

_____

_____

A What is the baptism for the dead (15:29)? What happens to people after they die? How can this message help a believer in Christ? How can it help an unbeliever?

MORE
for studying
other themes
in this section

B Compare our present bodies with our resurrection bodies (15:35–49). How are they similar? How are they different? What are some of the limitations of our physical bodies? How can we use our bodies to glorify God?

C What does it mean for us that Jesus is the "last Adam" (15:22, 45–49)?

D What will happen when Christ returns (15:50–54)? What can you do now to prepare for that event?

REFLECT
on your life

1 Who has made a significant difference in your life?

_____

_____

_____

_____

_____

_____

2 What did this person do that made such a difference?

_____

_____

_____

_____

_____

_____

READ
the passage

Read 1 Corinthians 16:1–24 and the following notes:

❏ 16:1–4   ❏ 16:13, 14   ❏ 16:19   ❏ 16:22   ❏ 16:24

3 According to this chapter, how were people involved in Paul's ministry or in ministry in general?

_____

_____

_____

_____

4 What do Paul's personal requests reveal about him (16:5–11)?

_____

_____

_____

_____

Paul seldom ministered alone. In all of his travels and missionary ventures, he was in the company of trusted and valued friends. Some of his lowest times came when he was isolated. In spite of Paul's great gifts and calling, he recognized his need for fellowship and support. He depended on others for help and encouragement. These supportive people were his partners in ministry. God calls all of us as Christians to be involved in ministry. We are partners together with Christ and other believers. How incredible to realize that God calls us to partnership in the building of his Kingdom!

REALIZE
the principle

5 What are the benefits of being involved with other people in ministry?

_____

_____

_____

_____

_____

6 What consequences might there be for people who minister by themselves?

_____

_____

_____

_____

_____

7 What are some of the unique needs of ministry leaders?

_____

_____

_____

_____

_____

RESPOND
to the message

8 In what ministries do you have a support role?

_____

_____

_____

_____

_____

9 In what ministries do you have a leadership role?

_____

_____

_____

_____

_____

10 Who has been a part of a "life-support system" for you in your Christian life?

_____

_____

_____

_____

_____

11 How can the people of your church encourage and support those involved in leadership?

_____

_____

_____

_____

RESOLVE
to take action

12 What leaders in your church can you encourage or support—a pastor, a small group leader, elders, deacons, church school teachers, or others?

_____

_____

_____

13 Choose at least one person from the above list and write down how you will encourage him or her this week.

_____

_____

_____

_____

_____

A What do Paul's instructions to the Corinthians in 1 Corinthians 16:1–3 suggest about how Christians should give? What can you do to support God's work with your money?

B What do you learn about Paul's ministry from 1 Corinthians 16:5–9? Paul said that there was "a wide-open door for a great work" in Ephesus for him (16:9). What factors may have led him to conclude this? How might opposition affect your ministry for Christ?

C How did Paul end this difficult letter to the church at Corinth (16:19–24)? What can this teach us about confronting others with problems?

D Paul longed for the Lord's return (16:22). How did this affect his ministry? What effect does the promise of Christ's return have on your life?

MORE
for studying
other themes
in this section

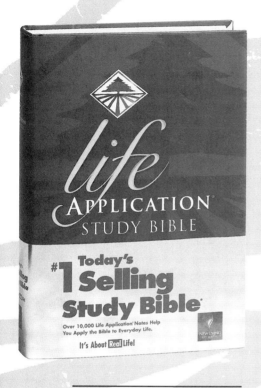

LIFE APPLICATION STUDY BIBLE

Applying God's Word to Life

Read it, and others will read it in you.

*The **Life Application Study Bible** gives you real answers for real life. Here are eight good reasons why it has all the answers you've been looking for – right at your fingertips.*

1. **Life Application Notes:** Over 10,000 notes help explain the Scriptures and challenge you to apply their truth to your life.

2. **Megathemes:** At the beginning of each book is a short study that tells you why the significant themes in each book are still important today.

3. **Personality Profiles:** You can benefit from the life experiences of the best-loved and most-despised characters of the Bible.

4. **Topical Index:** This provides you with instant access to Bible passages that address the topics on your mind right now!

5. **Bible Timelines:** These give you dates, names, events, and places at a glance.

6. **Blueprints:** Quickly discover what is covered in each book of the Bible by reading the outline or brief descriptions.

7. **Harmony of the Gospels:** Using a unique numbering system, the events from all four Gospels are harmonized into one chronological account.

8. **New Features:** Words of Christ in red letter, a dictionary/concordance, and daily reading plan are now included.

Plus: Book Introductions, Vital Statistics, Maps, and Charts!

Available in the New Living Translation, New International Version, and King James Version.

AT BOOKSTORES EVERYWHERE